CRIME
PUZZLES

Inspiring | Educating | Creating | Entertaining

Brimming with creative inspiration, how-to projects, and useful information to enrich your everyday life, Quarto Knows is a favorite destination for those pursuing their interests and passions. Visit our site and dig deeper with our books into your area of interest: Quarto Creates, Quarto Cooks, Quarto Homes, Quarto Lives, Quarto Drives, Quarto Explores, Quarto Gifts, or Quarto Kids.

© 2020 Quarto Publishing Group USA Inc.
Text © 2005 by Fair Winds Press

First Published in 2020 by Fair Winds Press, an imprint of The Quarto Group, 100 Cummings Center, Suite 265-D, Beverly, MA 01915, USA.
T (978) 282-9590 F (978) 283-2742 QuartoKnows.com

Fair Winds Press titles are also available at discount for retail, wholesale, promotional, and bulk purchase. For details, contact the Special Sales Manager by email at specialsales@quarto.com or by mail at The Quarto Group, Attn: Special Sales Manager, 100 Cummings Center, Suite 265-D, Beverly, MA 01915, USA.

24 23 22 21 20   1 2 3 4 5

ISBN: 978-1-59233-979-2

Digital edition published in 2020

Originally found under the following Library of Congress Cataloging-in-Publication Data

Vogt, M. Diane, 1952-
The little book of bathroom crime puzzles : two-minute forensic mysteries to challenge even the best amateur detectives! / M. Diane Vogt.
p. cm.
ISBN 1-59233-206-4
1.Puzzles. 2. Detective and mystery stories. I. Title.
GV1507.D4V64 2006
793.73--dc22
2006000440

Cover Design: Landers Miller Design
Interior Illustration and Layout: Landers Miller Design

Printed in China

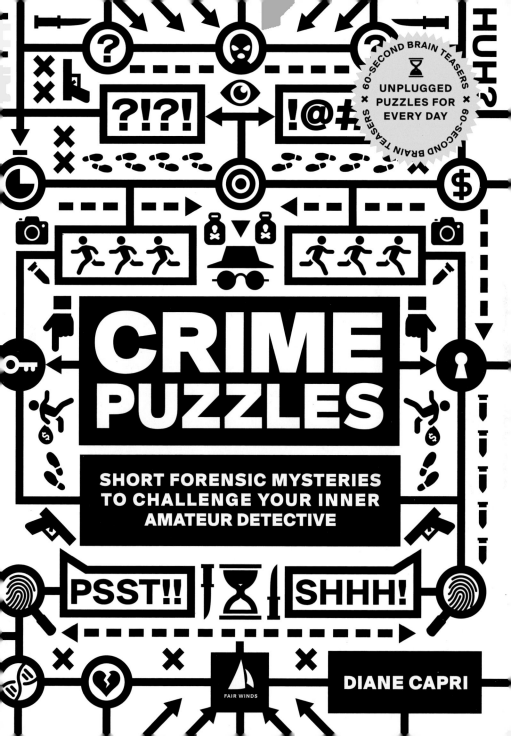

CONTENTS

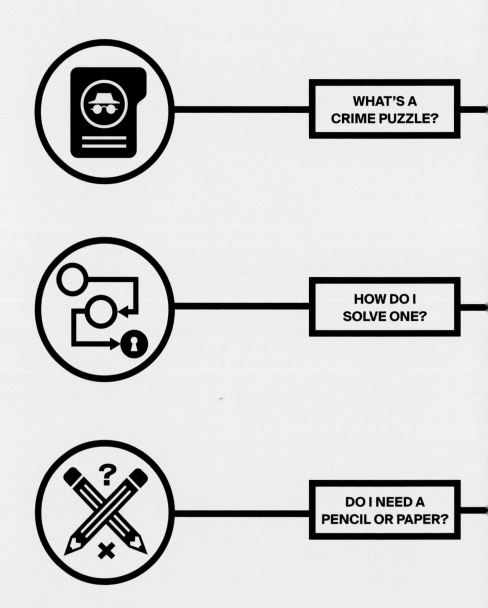

WHAT'S A CRIME PUZZLE?

HOW DO I SOLVE ONE?

DO I NEED A PENCIL OR PAPER?

INTRODUCTION

A crime puzzle is a short, captivating crime story that lets you play the detective. After each condensed tale of greed, revenge, or just plain depravity, you'll be faced with a difficult question related to the crime. It's up to you to crack the case using deductive reasoning and all the forensic details and clues in the story. The sixty-five crime puzzles that follow vary in terms of difficulty and are completely independent of one another. They can be done in any order, one at a time, or all in the same sitting. (If you find yourself addicted!)

First, read the crime story. As you're reading, look carefully for clues that might help you answer the puzzle question. Sometimes clues are hidden in a character's account of the crime, sometimes they manifest themselves as suspicious behavior and other times they're located in a description of physical evidence. Be on the lookout for lies, as they are often an indication that someone is concealing their guilt. If you're stuck, try to visualize the crime as it must have occurred and check it against the physical evidence and first-hand accounts. Not every puzzle question will ask you to identify the guilty party: some will challenge you to uncover the criminal's motive, determine cause of death, or explain how investigators nabbed the perpetrator.

No. The only tools you need are your keen sense of logic, your wits, and a close attention to detail. While it helps to know a little something about forensics, most of the stories can be solved by logic alone. Those who are forensically-challenged will find useful educational tidbits throughout so they can learn as they go!

THE PUZZLES

01 Short on Evidence

Theresa and Kathleen, two law students, were assigned an old case to investigate and appeal as a prerequisite to their graduation. The defendant, Martin Shine, had been convicted twice. His first trial, fifteen years earlier, resulted in a guilty verdict. He was sentenced to death. An appeal a year later resulted in a new trial where he was convicted again and sentenced to life in prison.

Yet, Shine continued to maintain his innocence. The women knew that if they could somehow prove Shine's innocence, or get him a new trial, they would not only have served the judicial system they wanted to participate in, but also save another human life and get an excellent grade on the project. Perhaps good enough to score a job offer from one of the prestigious firms they coveted.

"Come on, Kath," Theresa said, late one night, after they'd been working on the case for several days straight. "You know this guy isn't getting out."

"But he's innocent."

Theresa snorted. "Yeah, right. That's what they all say."

"But it could be true," Kathleen replied. "And we have to write the appeal anyway, so we might as well explore all the avenues. We need new evidence."

Kathleen flipped through the crime scene photos again, looking closely at the knife, the position of the body, and the surrounding bloody furniture. "What can we ask for that hasn't been done?"

Theresa raised her hand and rubbed her sore neck muscles. They'd pored over the old files, read the briefs and the transcripts, and examined the evidence until she could almost recite it in her sleep, if she ever got to sleep. "Okay," she said, weary, wanting to finish the assignment and be done. "Shine was convicted on bite mark evidence both times. In both trials, Shine's dentition was compared to a bite mark on the deceased's thigh, and the jury found a match."

"You know how controversial that evidence is! And she was wearing shorts, so the bite was through the fabric," Kathleen argued.

"The jury found the match conclusive."

"But they were swayed by the circumstantial evidence. He lived nearby, he was a customer of the bar where she was killed, and he'd been there that night."

Kathleen was way too invested in this assignment. She would never give up unless they found some new evidence to offer. Suddenly, it came to her: "The shorts!"

How could the victim's shorts help prove Shine's guilt or innocence?

CASE NUMBER

02

CASE NAME

Good
Neighbors

STATUS

☐ CLOSED ☐ OPEN

SOLUTION

SEE PAGE 106

Edna Mae Wittkop had lived in a cold weather climate all seven decades of her life, so she had learned to appreciate good neighbors. Her neighbor, Harry Timmons, had plowed the heavy snow from her driveway early this morning while she'd baked him a pie. The pie was still warm when she decided to deliver it.

She slipped her feet into a pair of heavy boots and threw on a down jacket, lifting the hood to cover her head. She settled her old glasses on her nose, pushed her hands into her mittens, lifted the pie and waddled out the kitchen door. Edna Mae made her way carefully down the freshly shoveled driveway and across the street.

Breathing raggedly, she rang Harry's doorbell. "Well I can't leave the pie outside," she said aloud. She struggled with her mittens, but managed to turn the knob and push the door open. "Yoo hoo! Harry! Are you here?" she called, huffing from exertion. She entered and stopped cold in her tracks.

A man knelt down next to Harry's still body. He looked up, stared at her for several seconds, and then bolted out the kitchen door.

When the ambulance and the sheriff finally arrived at the scene, Edna Mae told them all she knew.

"Harry Timmons was attacked," she explained, her voice unsteady.

When the sheriff pressed further, Edna Mae couldn't give him a good description of Harry's attacker. Why not?

03

Double Feature

The International Society of Identical Twins' annual convention met in Las Vegas. Society members Jeff and James were professional magicians. Along with their wives, members Susan and Sarah, they provided the entertainment. All four were identically dressed and used their identical appearance to enhance their illusions. The audience could not tell the twins apart and the act was a great success.

During their performance, an argument broke out. An angry magician grabbed the long, heavy knives and began to juggle them. He lost his concentration, dropped the knives and one landed on Sarah, stabbing her in the chest. Blood splattered all over his clothes. The audience roared with laughter, believing it part of the routine.

But Susan was outraged. "You killed my sister!" she screamed, and picked up a knife, threatening him. The second magician struggled with her, grabbed the knife and stabbed her in the neck. Blood pumped out of her carotid artery, drenching him. The unsuspecting audience laughed harder as the curtain was hurriedly lowered, hiding the grisly scene.

Mr. Penguin, the hotel manger, ambled over, holding his cell phone to his ear as he reported the incident. "No one touch anything here," he said to the people milling around backstage. "We need to preserve the scene and the evidence."

Detectives quickly discovered that Jeff and Sarah were having an affair and their spouses had learned about it for the first time on stage that night. Susan had been pregnant.

Watching the detectives lead the brothers away in handcuffs, while crime scene investigators collected blood samples and other evidence at the scene, Mr. Penguin told the worried association president, "They'll analyze the DNA and sort this out. These guys will be in prison very quickly."

But the CSI in charge said, "The only way to solve this mystery is to get those guys to confess."

Why?

04

Food for Thought

"Despite what you see on television, Evelyn, homicide is an easy job. You want work? Try directing traffic in the rain for an entire eight-hour shift," Jake said, while tossing a bag of cookies into his basket. He waved to the stock clerk who passed him and headed into the back room. Jake's feet hurt from standing on the hard pavement and his uniform stuck to his sweaty back. It was late, and he was tired. He just wanted to get the groceries and head home.

"Well, you don't have to be so cranky," Evelyn replied. "I'm just telling you that homicide detectives make more money than you do and we could use the extra cash, that's all."

Jake rounded the aisle and started up the next. He liked shopping late at night when there were no other customers in the store.

"Yeah, whatever," he said. "Those homicide guys, all they do is check out the victim's known associates, figure out where they've been in the past few days and they've got the murder solved. Any idiot can do that. No genius in it, that's all I'm sayin'."

Jake was losing his patience with his wife. She had been married to a cop for five years. She should know all this by now, he thought.

Evelyn could see that she was getting nowhere with her husband. "Forget I ever said anything. I'm gonna go use the little girl's room while you check out. Hopefully our credit card will go through this time."

While Jake was checking out, a nervous looking man wearing a T-shirt and jeans entered the convenience store. He pointed a gun at the cashier and ordered him to hand over the cash. When the thief had his money in hand, he shot Jake and the cashier dead so there would be no witnesses and then jumped into a car waiting in the parking lot. The shooter and the driver got away. The police found no fingerprints because the gunman wore gloves. The store had surveillance cameras, but unfortunately, there were no tapes in them to record the crime. The murder weapon was a common .38.

Evelyn was in a state of shock. When the homicide detective approached her, she said, "Jake told me your job is simple. You'll get this guy today, right?"

The detective gently explained that robbery murders like this one were frequently unsolved because they were more likely to be random crimes. This case might have gone unsolved too, if not for one person who was able to identify the killer's face.

Who was able to identify the killer?

CASE NUMBER

05

CASE NAME

Clean Sweep

STATUS

☐ CLOSED   ☐ OPEN

SOLUTION

SEE PAGE 107

Theresa fished the key out of her purse and opened the front door while Emelda gathered the cleaning supplies from the back of the van.

"Mrs. Fernandez said Chad would be here to clean the pool while we work today," Theresa said.

"I don't like him," Emelda replied. "He scares me."

Theresa shrugged. "He killed that guy by accident and he's done his time." She walked straight through from the front door to the kitchen and loaded the dishwasher.

Emelda headed toward the bedrooms. "Once a killer, always a killer."

"If you ask me, Mrs. Fernandez is the one you should really be scared of," said Theresa. "That lady would sell her own grandmother. Mr. Fernandez tells me all the horrible things she does to drive him crazy."

Emelda poked her head around the corner and gave Theresa a long, hard warning stare. Mr. Fernandez and Theresa were having more and more of these private talks. Emelda was worried that they were going to lose their jobs if Mrs. Fernandez found out. Theresa ignored her.

The two women worked steadily, cleaning the house from top to bottom. Four hours later, the home was spotless but Chad had not arrived. Emelda was disgusted. "We can't wait here all day. We've got two more houses to clean before I pick up my daughter after school."

Theresa kneaded her forehead with her fingers, wincing at the migraine. "You go ahead. I'll just meet up with you when he gets here."

"Are you sure? I don't like leaving you here alone with him."

Theresa nodded, waving Emelda out the door. "It's fine. You'll just be up the street."

When Theresa didn't show up at the next house, Emelda did the work by herself. At the third house, Emelda began to worry. She called Theresa at 3:15p.m., but the cellphone kicked into voicemail after just a few rings. She left a message: "Theresa, where are you? I'm gonna finish the Smyth's house and then go get my daughter. I'll see you tomorrow."

Mrs. Fernandez returned home to a sparkling clean house at 6:00 p.m. When she walked to the backyard, she saw Theresa's body floating in the dirty pool. She brought her hands to her mouth in horror. "Oh, Chad! What did you do?"

When the police finally arrived, they pulled Theresa's body out of the pool. Among the belongings they found in her pockets were her house keys, her dead cellphone, and an empty change purse.

When the police located Chad and brought him in for questioning, he told them that he had arrived at 3:00 p.m., saw Theresa's body in the pool and took off, fearing that he'd be blamed.

Had Theresa accidentally fallen into the pool?

06

Love Crazy

I think she's our killer," Jerry said. He put a couple of coins in the vending machine and waited while the cup dropped, then the coffee. He raised his eyebrows, his way of offering to buy her a cup.

Linda shook her head in disgust, folding her arms over her chest. "You're such a cynic, you know that? This woman is grieving the loss of both parents right now."

"Look, she met a mysterious guy at her mother's funeral."

"So?"

"And according to several peoples' accounts, she was flirting with him. She later searched for him, but couldn't find him."

"That only means she wanted a date; it doesn't mean she's a killer." Linda was determined not to lose this argument. They had bet five bucks on the outcome.

"Flirting? At her mother's funeral?" Now it was Jerry's turn to be disgusted. "There's something weird going on there. That doesn't sound like the behavior of someone who's emotionally stable."

"Maybe the tall, dark stranger is our guy," suggested Linda. "Maybe he was using her to get to her father."

"Doubtful. I admit he's been tough to locate, but there's just no motive there."

They walked down the hallway to the psychiatrist's office. "Let's just wait and see what the doc says before we arrest her for her father's murder, okay?" Linda pushed the door open, allowing Jerry to walk in first.

Dr. James was waiting for them. He tapped the manila folder on his desk containing the suspect's medical chart with his glasses. "Sorry, Linda. This girl has a long history of psychopathic behavior—she was serving her own interest. She killed her father. No doubt about it."

Linda was amazed. "But why would she kill her father right after her mother died?"·

What was the woman's motive?

07 False Impressions

Dressed in cashmere, silk and Italian leather from head to meticulously shined toe, Mark stepped out of the limousine in front of the most exclusive private club in the city. Two beautiful women exited the car and followed close behind. The doorman was new.

"What's your name?" Mark asked, reaching into his pocket.

"Frank Jones," the man responded, opening the heavy mahogany door.

Mark removed a crisp bill from his gold money clip and held it up between two fingers, like a cigarette. "I'm Mark Hudson. I'll give you fifty dollars to remember my name."

"Thank you, Mr. Hudson," Frank said, smiling as he glanced down at Honest Abe and palmed the cash.

Mark flashed his bright teeth in a distorted smile as he entered the club, his entourage close behind.

Mark's chauffeur stood just a few feet away looking bored. After the door closed, Mr. Hudson safely inside and out of hearing, he said, "Don't look so impressed. The guy's not as cool as he seems."

"I don't care how cool he is as long as he's rich!"

Frank pocketed the bill and straightened his uniform.

"He'll also be back in prison in no time," said the chauffeur.

"How would you know?" the doorman asked.

Why does Mr. Hudson's chauffeur think he's prison bound?

08 Little Footprints

Long after midnight, Eric awakened from a sound sleep, amazed to find himself in the poolside lounger. He felt disoriented at first, until he remembered that he and his wife, Brenda, had been sitting outside, a bottle of tequila between them, telling jokes and drinking shots. The phone rang about 10:00 p.m. It was their teenaged daughter calling from her cell.

Kelly had been upset. Her boyfriend apparently broke up with her because Brenda wouldn't let her go to tonight's football game with him. Kelly asked her mother to go inside the house so that their conversation could be private. Brenda laughed and staggered out of her own lounger. Her speech was slurred when she told Kelly, "Okay, honey, but Dad knows how boys are, too." He'd smiled at her, poured himself another shot, and paid no more attention as Brenda, carrying the cordless phone, padded barefoot into the kitchen.

"I must have passed out," he mumbled to himself now. When he stood up, his head pounded mercilessly. "Hafta pay the piper." He looked down at his shoes until the lounger stopped spinning, steadied himself, and went inside calling, "Brenda? Brenda?" She didn't answer.

Eric stopped abruptly just inside the archway separating the kitchen from the foyer. Brenda lay stretched out flat on her back near the bottom of the stairs. Blood covered her face and pooled around her body on the floor. Eric looked down and saw he was standing in his wife's blood and noticed bloody footprints on the floor around the body.

He rushed over to Brenda and felt for a pulse. There was none. He moved her body slightly. She was laying on the heavy doorstop that normally rested near the front door, shaped like a pig, for good luck. The pig's sharp, pointed ears were covered in blood, too.

Brenda's blood had congealed into a sticky mess. The phone lay near her outstretched right hand. Eric picked it up, dialed the emergency phone number, and while staring at his wife's bare, white feet, reported, "Help! My wife's bleeding. She's hurt!"

But Brenda was more than hurt; she was dead. When the police finally arrived, they found six deep lacerations on the back and sides of Brenda's scalp that matched the shape of the pig's ears.

Was Brenda murdered?

CASE NUMBER

CASE NAME

STATUS

☐ CLOSED ☐ OPEN

SOLUTION

SEE PAGE 108

09

Smoke Signals

The neighbors gathered on the street outside, attracted like moths to light bulbs, watching with mixed horror and fascination as the firefighters battled the blaze in the front half of the home. The area had been in transition just a few years ago, but now, the tiny houses, stuffed in like sardines on lots too small to hold a double wide trailer, were frighteningly close to the mesmerizing fire.

Bill put his arm around Lisa and held her close. "I wonder if he's okay," she said.

He shrugged. "It depends on where he was in the house. Since the bedroom is in the back, maybe he's all right."

The house had been the only real asset the owners possessed, and it was heavily mortgaged.

"I know his wife's out of town," said Lisa, "but I saw him about an hour ago, taking out the trash. How can this be happening?"

A firefighter emerged from the front door with the family canary squawking in his cage. He handed the cage to Bill. "Can you care for the bird until the wife comes home?"

"Of course," Bill responded. He didn't know how his neighbor could sleep through a fire with that damn bird in his bedroom. The bird was loud enough to keep Bill up at night. Canaries are only supposed to sing in the morning, but this one squawked constantly.

Just then, EMS workers came out the front door with a body on a stretcher. Lisa's stomach turned when she saw the lifeless remains of her neighbor.

"Found him in bed," he heard one of the firefighters tell the EMS guy.

Bill stared. The old guy didn't smoke, but his trophy wife often puffed obscenely on a fat cigar. She was too proud of the home, he thought, to have set the blaze intentionally.

"What a horrible way to die," Lisa said quietly to Bill. "It must have been smoke inhalation because the body doesn't look burned or anything."

"He didn't die of smoke inhalation," Bill suddenly blurted out. "He was dead before the fire even started."

What brought Bill to this conclusion?

CASE NUMBER

10

CASE NAME

Hanging by a Thread

STATUS

☐ CLOSED   ☐ OPEN

SOLUTION

SEE PAGE 109

Jennifer reported the burglary right away. She had come home from work to find that some of her small electronics and all her jewelry had been stolen. She found her Persian cat, Jinx, hiding under her bed, scared half to death.

Officer Danes soon arrived at the house to make a report and found Jennifer in a panic. She was supposed to pick up her son at his game, but she could only focus on one thing right now. Besides, when she'd dropped Tim off, the coach told her they'd be starting a little late because the opposing team's pitcher wasn't there yet. "This has never happened to me before," she stammered as Officer Danes surveyed the house for evidence. "Who would do this?"

"Someone who doesn't like you very much, I'm guessing. Mind if I take a look around?"

She shook her head and picked up the phone to call her ex-husband, John. He worked the overnight shift at the post office, but he might be able to swing by the park and pick up Tim before his shift started. There was no answer. Big surprise. He was never around when she needed him.

"Find anything?" she asked, as she joined Officer Danes in the kitchen.

He showed her that the window to the back door had been broken. There were a few threads of material clinging to one of the shards of glass, where the burglar's sleeve must have caught as he unlocked the door from the inside. He also showed her an unusual shoeprint on the kitchen linoleum.

Just then, her son, Tim, raced in the door, his face flushed with pride. "Mom, Dad came to my game! The other team almost had to forfeit because one guy was late, but then they didn't. And I tagged a guy out at home. Coach said I'm the best catcher in the league." He stopped short when he saw the policeman.

"I'll leave you two alone, take the evidence down to the lab and see what I can find out."

Officer Danes brought the fabric sample back to the station where it underwent a process called pyrolysis. The fibers were burnt and the gases produced identified the fibers as 100 percent polyester.

Where did the fibers most likely come from?

11

Big Crime on Campus

SOLUTION
SEE PAGE 109

The foul stench blasted Veronica's nostrils the moment she opened the door. "It smells like someone died in here," she said just before she saw the scene of destruction. Her entire house was wrecked.

Veronica walked slowly from room to room, unbelieving, scanning upended furniture, food strewn everywhere, half-empty beer bottles, and crumpled bags of chips and pretzels. Half-eaten cheese cubes, apples, and pears littered the carpets. Popcorn kernels crunched underfoot as she paced along the tiles. She picked up the phone and called campus security.

"What happened here, Professor?" the officer asked when he arrived five minutes later.

"I don't know," she said. "Looks like a swarm of hard-drinking college students camped out for the two weeks I was off on spring break."

The officer took a quick look around the place. "We can probably get some fingerprints off these bottles and cans. But the kids who did this probably aren't in the system if they haven't been arrested before, so that won't help us much."

"What about DNA? Can't you match that?" Veronica asked.

He tisked, shook his head. "Everybody's an expert these days. DNA won't help without a suspect. Processing can take months, and it costs a fortune. There's not a lot of resources we can use here, I'm afraid."

A while later, Veronica's neighbor came across the street when he saw her crying on the front porch. "Who would do such a thing, Jeff? It hurts to think my students hate me so much!"

Jeff went into the house to see for himself. When he returned, he held up a bag of half-eaten cheese and a few apple slices.

"We'll soon find out," he told her.

What made Jeff so sure?

CASE NUMBER

CASE NAME

STATUS

☐ CLOSED ☐ OPEN

SOLUTION

SEE PAGE 109

12

Heir Apparent

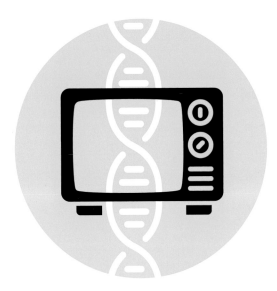

Olivia Sullivan was sorting through her grandmother's few belongings when she found the curious letter. Her grandmother had died last year at the ripe age of 101. One of the things her grandmother loved most in her old age was television. To her, it was nothing short of a miracle, the second greatest invention of the twentieth century, following ice cream available on request. But in those last few years, she began to show some signs of senility. She took her television shows seriously, almost too seriously, and sometimes forgot that they were not real life. One of the last times Olivia had seen her grandmother, they'd been watching an old movie together starring the famous actress, Virginia Haynes, who was murdered decades earlier.

"She doesn't look like her momma, does she?" her grandmother had asked. Olivia had nodded and smiled sweetly, but it saddened her to watch her grandmother lose her grip on reality. As if sensing Olivia's skepticism, her grandmother had turned her wrinkled face toward Olivia and stared out through those big, thick glasses: "You don't believe me? Ginny's momma and my momma were sisters. We're cousins, you know."

At the time it had seemed ridiculous. Olivia reread the wrinkled piece of paper in her hand. It was a letter from her great grandmother to her grandmother:

Dear Audette,

I hope you and Stan are well. We are looking forward to seeing you two during the holidays. The family is doing well. Dad got a new job in town and he seems to like it. Ginny came to visit last week and told us all about her big city adventures. Everyone asks about you and misses you a lot.

Love, Mama.

It now occurred to Olivia that grandmother may have been telling the truth. It seemed strange that she didn't know about it until now. Could she really have a famous relative? As days passed, Olivia became more and more curious about the truth. A friend told her that she could find out using maternal mitochondrial DNA, but that didn't seem possible since Virginia Haynes was long dead and her only living relative was a son, Harvey.

Was there any way for Olivia to determine if she was actually related to the famous actress?

CASE NUMBER

13

CASE NAME

Gambling Man

STATUS

☐ CLOSED ☐ OPEN

SOLUTION

SEE PAGE 110

The young victim lay on the dusty driveway of the casino, his eyes clouded over with death, blood congealed around the bullet hole in his chest. This was the third fatal shooting outside the casino in the span of two weeks. Officer Clark was pretty sure he had a serial killer on his hands.

Chief Joe Rainwater welcomed Officer Clark into his office. His tribe's casino, located in the middle of a sparsely populated Midwestern state, was an amazing cash machine. The Chief was astounded at the amount of money generated for the tribe. Last year, the casino provided jobs for his people, health care, even the money to start scholarships for college educations. They donated two new buses to the local elementary school and gave generously to various charities. After all of that, when they divided the profits, every member of the tribe over the age of 18 received almost $90,000 tax free. Younger members received $30,000, which their parents were encouraged to invest for the future. But the more members of the tribe there were to share the money with, the less each member received.

"We get a lot of people trying to rip us off," said the Chief.

His assistant, Sally Eagle, explained, "The local library's genetic research facility has been overrun by people wanting to prove they are related to a member of the tribe and deserve some of our money. About twice a week, we have to investigate claims but most of them are false. All three victims had recently submitted claims. Here's their paperwork."

The officer glanced down at the report. "Who has access to all of these claims?" he asked.

"Besides Sally and me, only workers at the research facility have access. You don't think one of our people would do this, do you?" asked the Chief.

"Maybe someone was trying to weed out the imposters in their own way. All three of these applicants had blue eyes, so the killer would have known that their applications were a joke. That must have been his reason for choosing them as victims."

Sally shook her head. "The DNA results came back on this last victim: He is a legitimate member of the tribe."

How is that possible?

14

Cold Comfort

Louise was bundled in wool from her head to her toes when she struggled out of her car. Despite the cold, her ninety-year-old neighbor was walking along the sidewalk headed away from her home. A baseball cap covered his thinning grey hair, but his ears were bright red. He had to be crazy to be out in this weather.

"Hey, Sam!" she called, but he walked on. Maybe he didn't hear me, she thought. She knelt down and pulled the newspaper out of the bushes where the delivery boy inevitably tossed it. He was a good kid who volunteered at the local shelter, but he had a really bad arm. Inside, the house was cold, too. She turned up the thermostat and lit the wood she'd laid in the fireplace this morning.

She knelt in front of the crackling fire, holding her hands toward it for warmth. Glancing down, Louise noticed a wiry white hair on the green carpet. She reached over and picked it up, tossed it into the fireplace, and continued to warm herself.

Once the fire was burning well, Louise moved into the kitchen. She saw another white hair in the sink. She turned on the water and washed it down the drain and wrote *hair color* down on her ever present grocery list.

As she and the old farmhouse began to warm, Louise ignored the whistling of the wind through the cracks in the walls. Feeling old, she hung her coat and trudged up the stairs to change. She walked into her bedroom, stopped and gasped. Chaos reigned in her normally well ordered enclave. Drawers pulled open, contents strewn everywhere, clothing thrown on the floor. Louise hurried to the closet where the missing clothes revealed a clear view of the open wall safe. She looked frantically into its empty depths, which once held her precious heirlooms and now held a single strand of white hair.

Local police put the hair under a microscope and found triangular-shaped scale patterns on the cuticle. These spinous scales helped point the police in the right direction.

Who broke into Louise's house?

15 Shocking Evidence

June, a defense lawyer for S&E Heaters, was thwarted at every turn by the one fact that she could not change: The plaintiff's lawyer knew more about his client's case than she did. The case was a serious one and June's client stood to lose millions unless she could prove that their product, a hot water heater, was not at fault in the electrocution death of Mr. Edwards.

When Mr. Edwards was electrocuted two years ago, the paramedics thought it was an accidental death. They'd taken the body to the medical examiner (ME), who checked the ocular fluid and learned that Mr. Edwards had been intoxicated when he stuck a metal screwdriver into his hot water heater while standing barefoot on wet carpet. For the defense, that was good news. It meant Mr. Edwards was negligent and his death wasn't caused by a defective hot water heater.

But the medical examiner had screwed things up royally. He hadn't followed the rules about chain of custody of the evidence. Because he could not account for the location of the blood alcohol evidence at all times, it was possible that it had been tampered with. The plaintiff's lawyer successfully argued to exclude the evidence from the case. Because of that, June worried that her client would have to write the Edwards family a settlement check with lots of zeros.

"What are you moping about?" June's boss asked her.

She explained everything.

"You're overlooking something, aren't you?" he asked.

"What?"

"I see Mr. Edwards was an organ donor. And you know what that means."

June thought about it a while. Finally, her face lit up with comprehension.

What did June realize that made the case defensible?

CASE NUMBER

16

CASE NAME

Intoxicating Question

STATUS

☐ CLOSED ☐ OPEN

SOLUTION

SEE PAGE 111

The expert's deposition testimony was going south in a hurry. The defendant driver, a local pool champion, had left the tiny dive bar called the Happy Time Lounge at midnight. On his way home, he hit two pedestrians, putting one in the hospital and leaving one dead, but revived at the scene. The driver served eighteen months for reckless driving, but now the bar that had served him to the point of intoxication was being sued by the injured pedestrians. They took a break for the plaintiff's lawyer to confer with his witness. The stakes were high because the bar owner and his employees could also be charged with reckless endangerment and sent to prison if they served the driver when he was already intoxicated and then allowed him to drive.

"Come on, Dr. Stanton," said the plaintiff's lawyer. "There has got to be a way to estimate this guy's level of intoxication when he left the bar. He blew a .22 on the Breathalyzer after the accident. And we know he drove directly to the scene. Less than ten minutes had to have passed."

Dr. Stanton, a blood alcohol expert, listened to the tirade calmly. He'd heard it before. "Let me see if I can explain it this way, Albert. We can extrapolate the number of drinks this guy must have consumed prior to the time he hit those pedestrians based on his height, weight, and the breathalyzer results at the station afterward."

The lawyer nodded in agreement. "Right. But we need to prove that the bartender served him when he was *visibly* intoxicated. Can you say that?"

"Unfortunately, no."

"Why not?"

"Because I wasn't there. I can't say how he *appeared* to the bartender at the time they served him his last drink. Some habitual drinkers can have five or six drinks and still don't appear drunk."

Albert's frustration grew. "The defendant testified that every day after work, and the day of the accident, he was in the Happy Time Lounge from just after 6:00 p.m. drinking beers and playing pool. Witnesses claim that he was at least angry when he left. If he was uncharacteristically angry, isn't that as good as saying he was drunk? People often get more emotional when they're drunk, right?"

"That's not my area of expertise. Here's what I can testify to: When his blood alcohol level was .03 percent, he should have been giddy. When he reached .08 percent, he'd probably have had trouble with his motor skills, reaction time, and judgment. But would anyone have seen that? They say not."

"Wait a second," said Albert. "If the guy was angry for the reason I think he was, we might still be able to win this case."

Why does the lawyer think the defendant was angry that night?

CASE NUMBER

CASE NAME

STATUS

☐ CLOSED   ☐ OPEN

17

Sharp Reality

SOLUTION

SEE PAGE 111

Logan crept around the corner of Bud's house, moving carefully, but a bit unsteady. Logan had already consumed half a bottle of vodka while partying with friends and he was feeling drunk. Bud never locked his back door, and he kept the liquor in a cabinet nearby. Logan saw Bud put the bottle of vodka on the middle shelf when he looked through the window. By now, Bud would be passed out in the living room in front of the television, the way he spent every evening in the long, cold winter. Logan's plan was to enter the house by the back door, steal the vodka, and get home before Bud woke up.

The television show was one of those ridiculous reality programs. The volume was up loud enough to wake the dead, but Bud would be snoring right through it. Logan turned the doorknob slowly and pushed the squeaky door open wide enough to slip inside. His snow-covered boots left puddles on the floor, but old Bud would never notice. The entire house was a pigsty since his wife died, anyway.

A few more steps. A board creaked. Logan stopped, waited, heard nothing, and moved on. He opened the cabinet, reached in, and grabbed the vodka bottle. A slow smile widened his lips as he exclaimed quietly, "Yes!" He tipped the bottle up to sip.

Bright light flooded the room. Bud stood in the doorway, curly grey chest hairs poking through the open neck of his flannel robe. "Boy! Put that back!" he shouted.

Logan pulled out a pocketknife. "You stay away from me, old man!"

Bud charged at Logan, knocking him and the bottle to the ground and grabbing the knife. They struggled for a while on the floor. Bud had Logan pinned until Logan wrenched himself free and staggered out of the house, bleeding from a single wound in his chest.

Outside, Logan used his cellphone to dial the emergency number. "Help me," he wheezed. "Bud stabbed me in the chest."

Logan was taken to the hospital where emergency room doctors discovered an irregularly shaped wound, wider than it was deep, on one side of his chest. They recovered something from the wound, performed the surgery, and saved Logan's life.

Based on Logan's story once he recovered, and the substance doctors found in the wound, the police concluded that Bud did not stab Logan.

What did doctors find in the wound?

CASE NUMBER

CASE NAME

STATUS

☐ CLOSED   ☐ OPEN

SOLUTION

SEE PAGE 111

18

Where There's a Will

After a lengthy disability following a massive stroke in his sixties, Dr. Hindricks passed away. One week later, his potential beneficiaries gathered for the reading of his recent handwritten, or holographic, will. Two sturdy middle-aged daughters sat close together on the sofa, radiating hostility while the stunned old housekeeper and her nephew occupied a smaller loveseat across the room.

"But that can't be true!" the housekeeper exclaimed when told that Dr. Hindricks had left her nothing. "He promised! Let me see the will."

Cynthia, the oldest daughter, had been stingy all her life. She snapped, "What did you expect? You lived here, rent free, while he clothed and fed you for years. Why would he have left you anything?"

"He said he'd take care of me in his will," she answered, seeming older, more bewildered now. She buried her face in her nephew's sweater.

The nephew looked directly at the lawyer and said, "I witnessed Dr. Hindricks' will two years ago in your office. It was typed by your staff. This is not that will."

"It seems he had a change of heart after the stroke," explained the lawyer. "A man is entitled to change his mind, you know."

Melissa, the slightly younger and prettier daughter, spoke up: "He took care of you during his lifetime, dear. You never married, and have no children of your own. You don't need his money any more than we do. But this was daddy's decision and we can't argue with that."

The lawyer handed the will to the housekeeper. After just a brief perusal, she gasped. "But this is not Dr. Hindricks' handwriting at all! This will is a forgery!"

"That's crazy!" Melissa exclaimed.

"I know his handwriting like I know my own," said the housekeeper with conviction. She pulled an old letter of recommendation from her purse. "Here. Here is the proof I need. He wrote this for me three years ago when I moved out of his house."

Will the letter prove that the will is a forgery?

19

Black and Blues

It was a clear and sunny Sunday afternoon and Susan was headed to a family party. She checked her makeup in the rearview mirror before getting out of the car.

"Hi, honey," her father said, leaning in to kiss her on the cheek when he opened the door. She winced a little. He looked past her to the empty sidewalk. "Where's David?"

"Oh, he's resting at home. He was traveling the first half of the week, and he likes to catch up on the weekends," she told him as she breezed into the house. "Where's the party?"

"Everyone is out on the patio," her father answered.

When Susan opened the sliding glass door and walked onto the patio, her mischievous three-year-old nephew immediately doused her with a blast from his water cannon. The adults chuckled under their breath as water and makeup dripped down her face.

Susan saw that the other adults were wet and bedraggled themselves. With a big grin, her sister tossed her a towel. "Wipe yourself off and join the crowd. We all walked right into it."

Susan gently blotted the water from her face. When she finished, all of the adults were staring at the dark purple bruise on her cheek. Cheri gently touched Susan's face to examine the bruise, but her tone was hard. "How did this happen?"

Susan's father walked out onto the patio. His eyes grew wide when he saw what all the commotion was about.

"Oh, it's nothing. I walked into the side of a door when I was rushing around the other morning. You know how clumsy I am," she said.

"When was that?" Cheri asked.

"Tuesday. I had a big meeting to make. So what kind of cake did we get mom this year?" she asked, trying to change the subject.

Her father rushed into the house and Susan rushed after him. He was dialing the police.

"I can't believe you're covering for him. I warned David not to hit you again."

"Dad, I'm not lying. I got this bruise on my own. He wouldn't do this to me."

"I know for a fact that you are lying. You couldn't have gotten that bruise on Tuesday," her father answered. Just then the dispatcher picked up on the other end. "Yes, I'd like to report an incident of domestic abuse."

How did Susan's father know for sure that she was lying?

20

The Convenient Thief

The convenience store manager entered through the front door and approached Philip, the young man who worked the night shift, startling him. "Uh, hi, Mr. Alfred. What are you doing here?"

Mr. Alfred looked around the store, noticed a couple of Philip's friends hanging around the video games, drinking sodas and munching snacks. It was against store policy for Philip to have friends on the premises during business hours. "Needed a couple of things and I don't live far from here." Slowly, Mr. Alfred approached the cooler, selected milk and eggs, then collected chips and soda, observing Philip surreptitiously. Philip slouched against the counter. When Mr. Alfred returned to the counter, he unloaded his arms, placing the items deliberately and watching Philip's reaction.

"I also wanted to tell you that we've had some thefts from the store lately," said Mr. Alfred. "Do you know anything about that?"

Philip shook his head and rubbed his nose. He couldn't stand Mr. Alfred. He was always pushing him to work extra hours and wouldn't switch him to the day shift like he wanted. He lifted each of his manager's items and scanned the bar code.

"I'm thinking you or your friends might be responsible," Mr. Alfred said, pulling a credit card from his wallet and tapping it on the counter. He was sick of these punk kids and their attitude problems.

"No way, Mr. Alfred! I don't even eat junk food because when I do, I break out." He heard his friend Jimmy stifle a laugh.

Mr. Alfred stared straight into Philip's pimpled face: "I think you're lying," he said.

Was Philip telling the truth?

CASE NUMBER

CASE NAME

STATUS

☐ CLOSED   ☐ OPEN

SOLUTION

SEE PAGE 112

21

Twin Terrors

Once the classroom quieted down, Professor Mitchell, who lectured the undergraduate class twice a week on scientific matters, began. Today's lesson involved fingerprint analysis, something most of the students were familiar with from watching television crime shows.

"Perhaps you recall the case last spring involving the disappearance of a young woman while participating in a class trip to one of the Caribbean islands?" He heard murmurs of assent from the audience. "You'll recall that she was last seen in a bar with her classmates. She had been there for several hours, dancing and drinking, before she left with two young men—identical twins, native to the island. She was seen with one of the men on the beach a couple of hours before her body was discovered in the same location. The question was whether one of the twins was her killer, and if so, which one?"

Sharon raised her hand. "Didn't they find a couple of beer bottles on the beach where some other partiers discovered the body?"

Jason blurted out, "Yeah, that's right. They found two beer bottles. One of them had her finger prints on it and the other one had one of the guy's saliva and prints."

Flashing Jason an annoyed look, Sharon continued, "As I was saying, the bottle that had the guy's saliva on it was the murder weapon."

Jason interrupted again. "And that's how they identified the killer. He was dumb, man. Really dumb."

Professor Mitchell regained control of the discussion to avoid another of Jason and Sharon's legendary squabbles. "That's right. Authorities found the murder weapon and it contained saliva sufficient for DNA analysis."

Jason interjected. "But DNA could only show that one of the twins committed the crime."

Sharon gloated, "Right. Identical twins have identical DNA."

"So what was it that did the killer in?" asked the professor.

How did police identify which of the twins killed the young woman?

22

Dead Man Gawking

The amateur photographer stood to one side of the corpse, taking digital photographs of the scene when a gawker approached. "So what happened here, man?" he asked, watching blood ooze out of the victim's chest.

"I don't know exactly. When I got here, the guy was already dead. I think a gunshot wound or something," the photographer said.

"Friend of yours?" the gawker said, swiping a shaky hand over his own chest, as if there might be a hole there, too.

"Nah. Never saw him before. I'm thinking I can sell these pictures to the paper."

"How long has he been lying there?"

Framing the body and surrounding area in the viewfinder of his camera, slightly breathless from the excitement of discovering the bloody scene, the photographer said, "About half an hour, maybe. I didn't hear any shots, and I was sitting in the café across the street having coffee and reading the paper. When I walked over here and saw the body, I called the emergency phone number on my cell."

Now, police officers and emergency medical personnel surrounded the area like ants at a picnic. The two guys watched as the body was quickly loaded onto a stretcher while blood oozed out of his mouth.

"The dude ain't dead, man," the gawker told the photographer.

How did he know?

CASE NUMBER

23

CASE NAME

The Long Goodbye

STATUS

☐ CLOSED ☐ OPEN

SOLUTION

SEE PAGE 113

Jenny entered the library, seeking just the right information. The problem was a tricky one. She watched enough of those television crime shows to know that. She approached the young man behind the research desk. "I wonder, could you show me where I can find information on poisons?"

"What kind of poisons?" he asked her with a nice smile. "Too many bugs on your rose bushes?"

"Uh, no. I'm a mystery writer and I want to use an untraceable poison in one of my books to kill off a bad guy," she told him, using the lie she'd rehearsed in front of the mirror at home.

Even though Max had one foot in the grave and the other on a banana peel, Jenny knew his kids would blame her for his death. Unless he died of natural causes, they'd suspect her and demand an autopsy. After all, even under the terms of the prenuptial agreement, she'd get a life estate in the house and its contents, and a pretty substantial sum of money, too. So the poison had to be untraceable.

Two hours later, Jenny was still mired in the section of the library containing reference works for writers. It seemed that most poisons were traceable. But there was one that seemed to fit the bill. Jenny closed the books, reshelved them, and headed home after stopping at the drug store to refill Max's medication and pick up a few things for herself.

She came home to find Max asleep in bed. She changed into sweats, dilly dallied around the house, painted and repainted her nails, and finally helped Max with his evening medications, as usual. She slept restlessly that night, with Max in the next room. She could hear his wheezing through the walls. Max was old, he suffered from cardiac problems, and he had asthma. How long could he live, anyway?

Max suffered a seizure during the night. Jenny called the emergency phone number. Max was taken to the hospital, treated for his seizures and shortness of breath and released. Over the next three months, Max's condition deteriorated drastically. He became weaker, more confused, and suffered from headaches and dizziness. When he was awake, his behavior was erratic and bizarre.

During the last visit from his children, Max died. Jenny jumped for joy, but she waited until Max's kids were out of sight to begin packing for her Grand Cayman vacation.

If not for the faint smell of almonds present during autopsy, the medical examiner might never have known there was foul play.

What had Jenny used to kill Max?

The fire alarm sounded in the fire station at three in the morning. The dry, old wooden boarding house was in flames before they arrived and burned long into the night. Firefighters were able to tamp down the flames and keep the fire from spreading to the adjacent buildings. When daybreak revealed the charred remains of the sleeping quarters, most of the residents were huddled together on the street, wrapped in blankets provided by neighbors, and giddy to be alive, thankful for the smoke detectors and the fire alarms. It didn't take long for the fire chief to determine that an accelerant had been used to start the fire and to make it burn hotter. The fire was arson.

Chief Franks walked along the street, a clipboard in his hand, asking each of the residents their names and room numbers, accounting for survivors. He checked off the names as they were revealed to him until he reached the end of the list, and the last of the survivors.

Two names remained unchecked.

"Manny Sams? Corrine Black?" he called out as he walked up and down the sidewalk.

A young woman placed her hand on his arm. "I know Manny and Corrine. Their bedroom was Room 6, in the back, near the bathroom and the back stairs."

"When did you see them last?" he asked.

"They were meeting some friends at the Red Dragon about eight, and I never saw them come back. Maybe they weren't home?" she said, sounding hopeful and fearful at the same time. Her bottom lip quivered.

Chief Franks approached the lead firefighter, asking him to recheck the back hallway. They found the bodies of the two students lying flat on the floor not far from the door to their bedroom. Both were in the hallway, face down. Their heads were close to the open bathroom window, only five feet from the back entrance stairs.

Chief Franks walked into their bedroom and noticed the bed had been slept in. "We'll know for sure at autopsy, but it looks like they made the classic mistake," Chief Franks said. "And we need to find the killer. Arson producing death is murder."

On autopsy, both students were found to have excessive soot in the airway passages and blood samples showed carbon monoxide.

What mistake did the students make?

CASE NUMBER

25

CASE NAME

Where's
Waldo?

STATUS

☐ CLOSED ☐ OPEN

SOLUTION

SEE PAGE 114

I can't believe Waldo's been gone for a year," Melvin whispered to Elmer as they waited for the memorial service for their buddy to begin. "It's gotta be hard on his family."

"Yeah, drowning in a lake on Father's Day isn't exactly the way I want to go." Elmer looked up toward the front row of the church where Waldo's widow and two adult sons waited, heads bowed, for the mourners to be seated.

"I can't believe they never found his body. And it was an inland lake. All they got was an empty boat with no signs of foul play." Melvin looked around to make sure no one was close enough to hear: "He had a mistress, you know. She moved away right after he died. Probably couldn't stand being reminded of him everywhere she went."

The organist began to play an old gospel hymn and the pastor asked the congregation to rise and sing along. One of Waldo's sons wrapped his arm around his wife's shoulder while she lifted a handkerchief to her eyes.

Elmer got a funny look on his face. "Didn't Waldo's house get broken into about a week before his death?"

"Yeah, they took just about everything of value. Opened the safes, found all the jewelry—even plucked the antique paintings right off the walls."

"This is going to sound crazy, Melvin, but I'm starting to think that Waldo is still alive."

"What on earth would make you think that?"

Why does Elmer think Waldo is still alive?

26

Helping Husband

Nettie lay on the sofa, a cold compress in one hand and a lit cigarette in the other. Her husband came in and sat next to her. He took the cigarette from her hand and put it out in the ashtray.

"Still having that migraine, hon?" he asked.

She didn't open her eyes, but patted his hand, to reassure him. "I just feel so tired. I ache all over. And my headache just keeps getting worse."

Joe Sr. took the compress to the kitchen and refreshed it, bringing along a glass of cool tea. He replaced the compress. He offered her the glass. She drank a few sips, and he encouraged her to finish it all. "When's the last time you took something?"

"About an hour ago, I guess. But the pain is getting stronger, not weaker."

"Do you want to go to the hospital? I tried to reach the doctor, but he must be on the golf course. I got the service," he said, trying not to alarm her.

Nettie kissed him and closed her eyes. "You and Joe Jr. go on to the park. Maybe pick up a movie while you're out. I'm sure I'll be better when you get back and we can order a pizza for dinner."

He didn't really want to leave her alone, but Joe Jr. was a noisy five year old who was about to burst with energy. "Okay. We'll be back in a couple of hours. I'll leave my cell on. Call me if you need anything."

He bent down to kiss her before they left.

When they returned three hours later, Nettie was dead. The doctor said her symptoms clearly revealed her cause of death, but an autopsy was performed because her death was unattended and outside the hospital. Following the autopsy, Joe Sr. was arrested and charged with murder.

What killed Nettie?

CASE NUMBER

CASE NAME

STATUS

☐ CLOSED   ☐ OPEN

SOLUTION

SEE PAGE 114

27

Hard-Hearted Woman

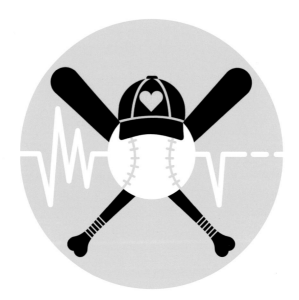

Marianne had had it with her ex-husband's maddening behavior. They'd been divorced for ten years and he still hadn't been able to come to terms with it.

"For years, I've been praying he'd find a girlfriend, start a new family, leave us alone," she fumed as she threw the kids' clothes into a suitcase. "Cut me some slack here, will you?" she implored.

The girls had been ordered by the court to visit their dad for the weekend, despite their almost desperate desire never to see their father again. "Steve has no interest in these kids. All he wants is to punish me. Well, I've had it! I'm done here! If he does one more outrageous thing, I'll kill him! Do you understand me?" The room remained silent.

Two hours later, Marianne fumed silently as she and her daughters sat in the stands while her ex-husband played shortstop for the local over-forty baseball team. He'd forgotten to arrange a sitter, and she couldn't simply leave the girls alone while he was out there reliving his childhood fantasy. *Maybe I could run him over with my car,* she thought.

Marianne wasn't paying close attention to the game, but Steve seemed a little slow out there. In the fourth inning, Mickey, Steve's long-time rival and the best batter in the league, was up to bat. He hit a line drive off the rookie pitcher's first pitch. Steve stood poised, glove out, but it hit him hard in the chest, knocking him to the ground.

"Gotcha!" Mickey shouted as he dropped the bat and ran to first base. Steve didn't get up.

"Oh, my God!" Marianne shouted, rushing from her seat down to the infield. Steve lay still, surrounded by his teammates. She knelt down over his still body and began to pat his cheeks with the flat of her hands. "Steve! Steve! Wake up!"

After a few seconds, Steve opened his eyes, grinned and said, "Gee, Marianne, I didn't know you cared."

Infuriated by his sarcasm, Marianne closed her hand into a fist and pounded on Steve's chest right where the ball had hit him moments before. "You are such a jerk!" She got up and stomped off the field.

Steve remained flat on the ground. After a minute or so, his teammates noticed he was still lying there. The coach walked over, knelt beside Steve's body, then looked up. "There's no pulse. He's dead."

Did Marianne kill Steve?

28

Strip Tease

The prostitute rang the bell three times before Roger eventually answered the door. He seemed a bit confused.

"Yes?" he said, running an open palm over his face, as if he were waking slowly from a deep sleep. His breath reeked of booze.

"I'm Ellie," she told him. "You called Rocky's Escort Service and Massage Parlor and asked for a home visit?" She'd driven more than an hour across town in bumper to bumper traffic, and she wasn't about to be sent away now that she'd arrived. This bozo had called for a massage and he was going to pay for it, one way or the other.

"Oh, right. Took you long enough. Come on in," he said as she followed him into the room. "Do you take credit cards?"

"Sure, honey. You bet. Give me the card and I'll call it in," she said between snaps of the wad of gum she'd stashed in her cheek. He handed her the card. Ellie dialed and spoke to someone, saying Roger wanted to pay with plastic. "What is it you want sugar? So we'll know what to charge you?"

"Oh, I want everything. The whole enchilada." Roger turned and headed down the hall while Ellie completed her phone call.

She joined him in the bedroom. Roger had disrobed. Ellie leaned against the doorframe and propped her foot against the doorjamb. She reached into her handbag and pulled out a lipstick, swiping it around her full mouth. She laid her purse on the dresser. It fell to the floor and its contents spilled onto the carpet. She casually put the contents back into her bag and asked Roger if he was ready.

"Sure, my muscles are really sore around my neck," he replied. "Do you do Shiatsu as well as Swedish massage?"

Ellie inwardly cursed her clumsiness, realizing she had blown her chance.

What went wrong?

CASE NUMBER

29

CASE NAME

Isolated
Incident

STATUS

☐ CLOSED   ☐ OPEN

SOLUTION

SEE PAGE 115

Andrew rode his bike around fallen tree limbs and scattered debris in the two-lane dirt road, delivering the afternoon papers in the rural neighborhood. Lightning and thunder had kept him awake half the night. The show was one of God's better ones, his dad said.

"Boy, that was some storm!" he said to himself again. There was no one else around to talk to. The homes were spread out on one or two-acre lots surrounding the inland lake where he lived. For some of these folks, Andrew was the only person they saw all day long, if they happened to miss the mail truck.

"Old Tommy! Hey! Old Tommy!" he shouted at the front door of Tom Stratton's place. The heavy oak door was open, and Andrew could see through the screen clear to the lake. He was already late, but his dad had made him promise to check on Old Tommy every day. The old gent was a bit senile and he lived alone, way out on the end of the road. Everybody in the community tried to watch out for him.

Andrew dropped his bike, opened the screen door, and walked through the musty house. Old Tommy kept it tidy enough, but the dust was as thick as pie crust. Andrew looked out the kitchen window into the backyard. He saw Old Tommy lying face down on the ground next to the clothesline. Andrew ran over to Old Tommy and saw that his shirt had been torn and there were angry red marks on his back. Someone had beaten Old Tommy to death!

He knew CPR, but when he reached Old Tommy, he felt for a pulse and didn't find any. Still, he ran back in the house and called his dad. "Come quick! They've killed Old Tommy!"

When the volunteer fire department arrived, Old Tommy couldn't be revived. The fire chief saw the red fernlike pattern across his back. "This was no beating," The fire chief said.

What killed Old Tommy?

CASE NUMBER

30

CASE NAME

All in the
Family

STATUS

☐ CLOSED ☐ OPEN

SOLUTION

SEE PAGE 115

The man dubbed Doctor Bandit for wearing a surgical mask, latex gloves, and green surgical scrubs to every robbery, struck again this afternoon at the U.S. Bank on South Twelfth Street," Brenda Starr reported on the noon news. "This surveillance tape from the bank's lobby camera shows the now familiar bandit walking directly up to the teller, thrusting a note and bag toward her, while holding a gun under his tunic. The teller gave Doctor Bandit $3,000 and he got away before the security team could catch him. Local banks have posted a reward of $25,000 for information that leads to the capture of Doctor Bandit. If you have any information, please call the number on your screen."

Ace watched the report from the lounge chair where he'd settled with his sandwich, a bag of chips and a large soft drink. He liked to come home for lunch. See the kids. Kiss the wife. He closed his eyes for a moment. Something about Doctor Bandit seemed familiar. What was it?

His brother, Deuce, called him a few minutes later. "Who does that Doctor Bandit guy look like to you?"

"I don't know. Who do you think it is?"

Before Deuce could answer, his other brother, Trey, ran into the living room. "Did you see that story about Doctor Bandit? I went online and read more about the robbery. A witness saw the guy's car: It's a green Chevy!"

Realization slowly began to dawn on Ace. "Oh, come on! Why would Dad do that, and where would he get the outfit?" He put Deuce on speakerphone.

Deuce said, "He's asked me for money several times in the past few months. I know he needs cash."

"And he's gone a lot. Come on, do you really think he's servicing poker video games in bars around the state? What kind of job is that for a sixty-four-year-old man?" Trey asked.

Ace thought long and hard about it. This was their dad they were talking about.

"Okay, he said he'd be back tomorrow. Let me talk to him then and sort this out."

Ace knocked on his father's door the next morning. Mr. Morris invited his son inside, and immediately put on a pot of coffee. Ace sat down and began gathering the courage to confront his dad. When his father handed him a steaming mug of coffee a few minutes later, Ace could see that both his hands were covered in small, red sores. There was no reason to ask at this point. He was sure his father was Doctor Bandit.

Why was Ace so sure?

31 Bubba's Fresh Fish

Early morning is the best time to fish, **Bubba thought. He'd been an early riser all his life, and there wasn't a whole lot to do at that hour besides fish out in the backwater. Nobody out there except him and the fish. His only competition was the alligators and Bubba was smarter than them.**

Bubba rolled out of bed, grabbed a cola from the fridge, and slipped on his old topsiders. Ten minutes flat, bed to boat. It takes years of practice to get fishing that quickly.

The summer sky lightened into a soft blue. Bubba thought he lived in paradise, for sure, and just maybe, in the best damn place on earth. What more did a man need? Besides breakfast, that is.

He cast his line again into the heavy reeds. He'd caught lots of big grouper here over the years. He got a strike. Quickly, he jerked the line, setting the hook, and began fighting with the fish. "Man, this oughta be tasty," he said aloud to the birds.

The fish didn't wiggle much after that, but Bubba had a bit of trouble reeling him in anyway because he kept getting caught in the weeds. Eyes closed, mouth watering with anticipation, Bubba gave one final tug and yanked his trophy up into the boat.

"What the hell?" His unexpected trophy, a cleanly severed human arm, lay on the floor of the boat. "Old Aggie strikes again," Bubba said, and returned home right away to call the police. Aggie was a local alligator blamed for the deaths of three different men.

But when Chief Parks arrived, he took ovne look at the arm and called the medical examiner. The arm had been severed near the shoulder. There was a double heart tattoo containing the names "Sam and Sally" on the forearm. "That ain't no alligator bite, Bubba. Nope. We got a murder on our hands."

How did the Chief know the arm wasn't bitten off by an alligator?

CASE NUMBER

CASE NAME

STATUS

32

Dumbfounded

☐ CLOSED   ☐ OPEN

SOLUTION

SEE PAGE 116

Walking slowly, Homer gave his brow a wipe: "Boy, it's hot," he said. "Some guy on the radio at the shelter said it was 117 for the fifth day in a row."

"It's supposed to be hot. We live in Arizona," Luther replied. They'd had the same exchange every day since the heatwave started. He was tired of talking about the weather.

Luther nudged his pal with an elbow, smiled his toothless grin, and teased, "Lookee there. It's Maggie. You should ask her out. She's rich you know. She's hefty, too. You like a big woman."

Maggie lay on the sidewalk, head propped on her bent arm, leaning against a shopping cart filled with empty liquor bottles and beer cans. "I saw her yesterday and she was acting real crazy, just like you like 'em."

"Aw, you're just jealous 'cause the women like me better'n you," Homer said, breathless, wiping his face with a dirty bandana. "She wasn't acting crazy, she was drunk. Besides, Maggie ain't rich. That's just some story."

The two men strolled on. When they were about fifty feet away, Luther started up again. "Man, ain't she a looker. You always liked them redheads. Go on over there and say howdy." He nudged Homer in the back, forcing him ahead a couple of stumbles.

Homer ambled a few more steps toward the woman. He thought she looked pretty peaceful with her eyes shut tight. "She's sleeping, Luther. You just be quiet and let the poor thing get some rest."

Luther looked more closely and saw dried blood on her face. "She ain't sleeping, you idiot. She's been murdered!"

**But the medical examiner disagreed. There were no entry wounds to be found.
What did the medical examiner rule as the cause of death?**

33

The Look of Death

Doug let his golden retriever out every morning to roam the property in the state park until she'd exhausted her instinct to explore. JoJo was a good dog and she always came home within the hour. Today, he'd glanced up at the clock to see that JoJo had been gone much longer. He stuck his head out the back door and called to her. Then he whistled. But she didn't respond.

"Couldn't you have picked a warmer morning to go on a long hike, girl?" he grumbled as he pulled on his jacket and his boots and tramped out into the marshy wetlands to find her. "JoJo," he called every few steps. He plodded toward the water's edge. JoJo was a retriever and she often returned with a dead animal of some kind in her mouth as a special present for him. He had a mini-graveyard behind the garage filled with ducks, possum, raccoons, and other animals that had died one way or another in the woods.

When he reached the shoreline, he saw JoJo about fifty yards down. She was sniffing something that had washed ashore, something much larger than a muskrat.

"JoJo," Doug called. She looked up, whimpered and wagged her tail, but didn't move away from her treasure.

Doug walked along the graveled shoreline until he was close enough to see what she'd found. He whistled in amazement. He slipped JoJo's leash onto the ring on her collar, opened up his cellphone and called the sheriff's office.

"We've got a floater, Paul," he told the dispatcher. "A woman. Head and limbs are pretty chewed up. No clothes. She's got a wedding band on her left hand. Looks like she's been in the water quite a while. She's got a tattoo of a butterfly on the small of her back."

When the crime team arrived, they took pictures of the dead woman's badly decomposed body. "You figure three weeks in the water?" Sheriff Mackie asked, his back to the victim. The sight made him nauseous. He became the sheriff of this sleepy berg because he didn't have any interest in solving homicides like this one.

After a visual inspection, the medical examiner said, "The water's pretty cold here this time of year. Could be longer. But that sounds about right."

"Well, I'll need some kind of an estimate to start checking missing persons reports," Sheriff Mackie told him, smoking a cigarette to control his nervousness. "Got anything on cause of death?"

The medical examiner turned the body over, very carefully. Now, the woman's face, what was left of it, was clearly visible.

"Looks pretty obvious to me," Doug said.

How did the woman die?

CASE NUMBER

CASE NAME

STATUS

☐ CLOSED   ☐ OPEN

SOLUTION

SEE PAGE 117

34

Guy Trouble

"You heard anything from Zack lately?" June asked casually, not really interested.

Tabitha shook her head, continuing to paw through the cute tops on the summer sale rack. "Not since we broke up two weeks ago. Why?"

June picked up a green tank with a monkey face on the front and held it up to Tabitha. She put it back. "Nobody's seen him for a few days. And I heard he was pretty upset about you dumping him again."

"Well, it's not like he didn't see it coming. We'd been fighting for months. I took him back before, and it just didn't work out. And he wouldn't leave me alone. What else could I do?" Tabitha pursed her lips into the pout she was famous for.

"Hire a hit man?" June joked just as her cellphone played a funky tune. She flipped it open. "What? Oh my God! When?" She listened a few more seconds, hung up, and turned to Tabitha. "You need to brace yourself: Zack's next door neighbor says he's dead!"

"What?" Tabitha's bewilderment and shock was plain on her face.

"They found his body in his garage. He shot himself in the head."

Tabitha gasped, both hands flew to cover her mouth, and she started to cry. "He told me he'd kill himself if I left him!"

They arrived at Zack's apartment to find the area sealed by authorities. They approached the officer blocking the entrance, explained who they were and why they were there. Detective Johnson interviewed Tabitha, who revealed the breakup and Zack's threat to kill himself.

A crime scene tech came out of the garage holding a plastic bag containing a suicide note, Zack's shoes and socks, a half-empty soda can, and a candy wrapper. "This is what we found in the garage," he told Detective Johnson.

Did Zack shoot himself?

CASE NUMBER

CASE NAME

STATUS

☐ CLOSED   ☐ OPEN

SOLUTION

SEE PAGE 117

35

Small Town Secrets

July 1905—Dr. Wilson's housekeeper, the comely Miss Button, piled her supplies on the counter. The pharmacist added them up aloud and wrote them down laboriously on a small card used to keep track of Dr. Wilson's account.

"You've got a pound of sugar at four cents, a dozen eggs at 14¢, and a pound of coffee at 15¢. That's a total of 33¢," Robert said.

Miss Button tisked and shook her head in consternation. "Robert, I swear, the way prices keep going up, poor Dr. Wilson will be broke before the year's out."

Robert laughed. He enjoyed flirting with the pretty young woman. Since Miss Button had come to work in his household, Dr. Wilson had become the envy of all the men in town. "Not likely. He makes close to $3,000 a year, I'll bet. Need anything else?"

Miss Button searched her memory. "Oh, yes. I almost forgot. Mrs. Wilson has been having a bit of stomach trouble. Dr. told me to pick up another vial of heroin, too."

Robert handed her the small vial and added the purchase to the book. "That's the fourth vial we've sold her this week. What kind of problems is she having?"

There was nothing juicier than gossip about one of the town's leading citizens.

"She's got the flu and it's been hanging on a while now. Yesterday, she started having some spasms and her fingers have turned a bit blue. She's out of her head a lot. I know he's worried about her."

Miss Button picked up her shopping bag.

"Let me know if this doesn't do the trick. Too many people in town have died from that flu epidemic. I sure hope Mrs. Wilson isn't one of them."

Robert had known Judy Wilson since their school days and had a bit of a crush on her back then, himself. True, she'd grown disagreeable, and many people didn't enjoy her company. But she did a lot of good deeds for the town.

Miss Button walked home. Although the doctor was one of the few people in town who owned a car, Miss Button refused to get in the contraption.

Mrs. Wilson was already drowsy at lunch time, but she ate her chicken soup and took the heroin before she settled in for another nap. Dr. Wilson came home for dinner, stopping in first to check on his wife. It was then he found that she'd stopped breathing quite a while before.

The death record showed that Judy Wilson died of influenza on the 16th of July, 1905. Was the death record accurate?

CASE NUMBER

36

CASE NAME

Drowning in Mystery

STATUS

☐ CLOSED   ☐ OPEN

SOLUTION

SEE PAGE 117

The ship's risk manager was nearly drowning in anxiety. When she'd finished playing the small snips of film retrieved from the ship's video surveillance cameras, she whined, "We have no idea what happened to Mr. Larson. His wife is frantic. You need to help me, Captain Bly!"

"Now is not the time to panic, Gloria."

Captain Bly famously kept his cool under pressure. This wasn't the first time a passenger had disappeared from his ship and it wouldn't be the last. Cruise ships were a cauldron of drunken revelers every night of the week. Some of them got left in port.

Gloria wrung her hands and paced the cabin.

"Mr. and Mrs. Larson are with us throughout the Mediterranean on their honeymoon. Last night, they drank two bottles of wine at dinner, and had several cocktails in the Under Sea Lounge. Witnesses say they stumbled back to their cabin with a bottle of vodka at about three in the morning" She took a deep breath and stated the rest in a rush, as if she wouldn't be able to finish otherwise. "Mrs. Larson passed out. When she woke up this morning, her husband had disappeared. There's blood everywhere!"

Gloria showed the captain two photos: One showed a bloody handprint on the four-foot railing outside his fourteenth deck cabin, and another showed a blood spotted awning on the balcony below. Captain Bly studied them carefully.

"It's a long way down and we're ten miles at sea from Kasudashi now," Gloria said. "No one could swim that far, especially if they were injured."

When she'd gone, the Captain reviewed her story and the collection of pictures she'd left. Three showed the couple in the Under Sea Lounge emptying their glasses of wine. Unfortunately, the ship did not have surveillance cameras in the cabin's hallways to identify those who entered the staterooms. In international waters, Captain Bly was responsible for justice. He called on Chief Capote, head of ship security.

"We cleaned up over four liters of blood in that cabin that matches Mr. Larson's blood type. We're running the DNA now." Chief Capote said. The captain showed Chief Capote one of the cabin photos Gloria had left.

"What did they have in this cooler?" he asked.

"Mrs. Larson said it was her insulin—she's diabetic."

"Did you check inside to verify that?" asked the captain.

"No."

Captain Bly thought for a few moments. "How much life insurance was there and who gets it?"

"Five million dollars, I'm told. The beneficiary is Mrs. Larson."

Captain Bly smiled. "Bring Mrs. Larson to my cabin. And check the cooler for traces of Mr. Larson's blood."

Who killed Mr. Larson?

CASE NUMBER

37

CASE NAME

Ill Will

STATUS

☐ CLOSED   ☐ OPEN

SOLUTION

SEE PAGE 118

The lawyer's face was grim as he informed the old woman's daughter that nothing had been bequeathed to her in the will. "But that can't be true!" Beatrice exclaimed. "I'm my mother's only heir. Who else would she leave her estate to? Mr. Scrivener?"

Beatrice hadn't been a very dutiful daughter, they both knew. Why, she hadn't seen Mrs. Cash at all in several years. Mr. Scrivener resisted telling her being left out of the will was the least she deserved after her shabby treatment of her mom during her last illness. Mr. Scrivener pushed the will across the table to allow Beatrice to examine it herself. "Mrs. Cash left her entire estate and money to Dr. Charity in recognition of his attentive care, I'm afraid."

Beatrice pulled her reading glasses out of her enormous handbag and examined the will, paragraph by paragraph. When she reached the signature page, she shouted n triumph. "Ha! This is not my mother's signature. She never used her first name. She hated the name Matilda. She always signed 'M. Louise Cash.' Not only didn't she sign this, but the forger didn't know her very well, did he?"

Mr. Scrivener contacted the police. With Beatrice's consent, they exhumed the body of Mrs. Cash and examined tissue samples. Indeed, Mrs. Cash had died not from illness, but from an overdose of morphine.

When Dr. Charity was confronted with the overdose, he seemed embarrassed. "I had hoped to spare you," he said to Beatrice. "Mrs. Cash suffered from a morphine addiction."

He printed out the earlier medical records from his computer. He displayed entries he had made regarding his suspicions that Mrs. Cash was addicted weeks and months prior to her death. "Poor thing. She was in so much pain, so confused at the end. She must have accidentally overdosed," he said. "I am so sorry, dear."

Beatrice snatched the medical records out of his hands. She examined the entries herself. Indeed, Dr. Charity had indicated his concerns. Beatrice's challenges to her mother's will would be dismissed unless she could think of a way to test the doctor's story.

"All we need is a strand of your mother's hair," said the police when she showed up at the station for the tenth time that week.

How could a strand of hair prove or disprove the doctor's story?

CASE NUMBER

38

CASE NAME

Bone of Contention

STATUS

☐ CLOSED ☐ OPEN

SOLUTION

SEE PAGE 118

Judy left work later than usual. With daylight savings time, it got dark so early. And tonight, a cold rain made the evening darker and more ominous. She buttoned her raincoat up to her chin and raised the collar. Opening a large umbrella, she stepped out into the sidewalk and started the sixteen-block walk home.

"Why didn't I get a ride with Ella?" she asked herself as she stepped over the puddles. Her shoes were quickly soaked by icy water and the wind blew wet gusts around her. She halted at the corner to wait for the green light, even though there was no traffic. It was not a fit night out for woman or beast, she thought.

A man dressed in a black rain slicker with a hood walked up and stood next to her. She could smell his fetid breath, he was so close, and the wind was blowing his odor toward her. She wrinkled her nose involuntarily. He turned to look at her, and she saw a bearded face, a bulbous nose, and square-framed glasses.

When the walk sign came on, Judy quickly stepped off the curb into a deep, cold puddle, rough at the edge. She lost her balance and fell onto the pavement. The umbrella jabbed her right side and her purse flew out of her hands, landing in the middle of the street.

"Dammit!" Judy exclaimed as tears of pain and frustration welled up in her eyes.

"Let me help you," said the stranger, bending toward her and reaching for her arm to help her up.

"I'm okay," she said and tried to stand on her own. When it became clear that she could barely walk, she looked back at the man desperate for his help. He put out his arm and helped her back onto the curb. He began steering her toward a dark doorway. She tried to pull in the other direction, but he resisted. His grip strengthened, which caused her to panic and struggle. Hours later, the police found her beaten and crumpled on the ground. An ambulance brought Judy to the hospital where she was treated for contusions, abrasions, and a sprained ankle.

When Judy gave a description of the man to a police sketch artist, he was able to create a very accurate picture of the criminal. The investigation gained momentum when police uncovered a few fingerprints on Judy's belt. It was plain luck that they hadn't been washed away by the rain. Her wounds also yielded enough saliva for DNA testing.

The DNA and fingerprints were run through the forensic and criminal databases and got a hit right away. "This can't be right," Detective Bayan said to his partner. "The DNA comes back to John Orr, but he's in prison and he's been there for five years!"

Detective Roberts said, "What about the fingerprints?"

"That's odd, too. The fingerprints are not Orr's at all," Detective Bayan replied. "How is that possible?"

They showed Judy a photo of John Orr and she did not recognize him.

Detective Roberts thought for a moment. "Let's find out if any of Orr's relatives has had leukemia, lymphoma, or any other type of blood disease."

Does the detective think that John Orr is Judy's assailant?

CASE NUMBER	CASE NAME	STATUS

39 Sticky Situation

STATUS

☐ CLOSED ☐ OPEN

SOLUTION

SEE PAGE 118

Billy ran up and slapped Frankie on the shoulder. "Tag! You're it!" he cried before he turned and ran away. Frankie squealed with outrage and headed after Billy as fast as he could run, up the small hill behind his house and out into the woods. He saw Billy standing stock still and ran into his back, full force, knocking him over. "You're it now!" he yelled.

He struggled under Frankie. "Get off me! Can't you see? We have to call the police!" When he finally got Frankie's attention, he rolled off him and looked in the direction he was pointing. Up ahead, under the shade of the trees, he saw a naked woman's body, all beat up. The woman's clothes were strewn around and Billy was now lying on top of a brown jacket. Frankie began to shake, and then to cry.

Police and crime scene investigators arrived at the grisly scene when Frankie's mother called them. The nude body of the murdered woman lay face down. She had been beaten severely. Her clothes were thrown around haphazardly and some items, like her shoes, were quite a distance from the body. CSIs collected the clothing and stashed each item in a separate evidence bag. They also located and photographed shoe prints in the dusty earth near the body. Another team searched the crime scene inch by inch looking for all forensic evidence left by the killer or killers.

Suddenly, Officer Smoak shouted, "Don't anyone touch her body!"

A startled CSI halted her hand half way to the woman's face, stood up, and glared at him. "And why not? I need to do my job if you want to catch the guy who did this."

"Right. But I want to try something here: The body is in the shade of the trees, obviously it hasn't been here too long so the evidence hasn't been contaminated by heat or excessive decomposition. We haven't had any rain or dew that would have washed away evidence. I've got equipment in my truck. I want to fume her," he explained.

"Her entire body?" CSI Jones was shocked at the idea. In the lab, they routinely used glue fumes to reveal finger prints and harden them into white whorls that could be photographed and compared to known criminals. But lifting fingerprints from human skin in the field was another matter entirely.

"It's worth a shot," Officer Smoak explained. "We have no witnesses and no identification on this victim. There's no way we're going to find out who killed her unless we have some good forensics."

They used plastic and PCV pipe to build a tent over the entire body. Then, they heated and fumed enough glue to fill the tent. When the tent was full of fumes and smoke, they waited. After a great display of patience, they found an unusual palm print on the woman's thigh, which they photographed and added to the crime file.

Could the palm print be used to locate a suspect?

CASE NUMBER

CASE NAME

STATUS

☐ CLOSED   ☐ OPEN

SOLUTION

SEE PAGE 119

40

Death Hits a Dinger

Scotty twisted his hands, bounced back and forth from one foot to another, bit his lip. He leaned his head against the small cell phone propped on his shoulder and waited for the cop to come back on the line.

"Okay, Mr. Scott. I'm sending a car to pick you up. They should be there any minute now."

Scotty dropped the phone. He bent down to pick it up, shaking so hard he couldn't get a grip on the small device with his big paw. A squad car drove up, two cops got out.

"Mr. Scott?" the young one asked.

"Yeah."

The older guy picked up Scotty's cell phone and held it to his ear. "We got him. Right. Be there in ten minutes."

Before he knew it, Scotty was in the back of the car headed to the station.

"Its okay, Mr. Scott," the older cop said. "We just need to get some more information from you. You told Officer Tims that your buddy killed a man last night?"

"That's right. Jack Emmett. He killed Lefty Allen." Scotty barely got the words out through his trembling lips.

"How do you know Jack killed him?"

"He called me. We ditched the baseball bat he killed Lefty with. Jack wanted me to help him get rid of Lefty's body." As soon as the words left his mouth, Scotty threw up all over the back seat of the squad car remembering the gory corpse he'd seen in Jack's living room.

The next day, police found Lefty's body hastily buried in Jack's backyard. The autopsy revealed two broken forearms and concluded that the cause of death was one of thirteen blows to the head with a blunt instrument.

Officer Tims arranged to have Jack Emmett arrested and questioned in the presence of his lawyer. Jack denied everything at first, until witnesses at Carter's Bar and Grille said that the two men had been drinking together the previous evening and had begun fighting in the parking lot after the bartender refused to serve them any more alcohol.

"But it was self defense! I swear! He came at me with the bat! When he swung at me and missed, I grabbed the bat from him. Then he came charging, so I swung and hit him in the head. What else could I do?" Jack claimed.

"He was beat up pretty bad," Officer Tims said, his skepticism plain.

"Well, I just lost it after that. I kept swinging. But he was already dead, anyway."

Was Jack telling the truth?

CASE NUMBER

41

CASE NAME

For Love
or Money

STATUS

☐ CLOSED ☐ OPEN

SOLUTION

SEE PAGE 119

Kate Black watched her reflection as she touched up her makeup. She was seated at her dressing table wearing her slip, stockings, and nothing else. She was glad to have a night off from worrying about the family's finances. Herbert, Kate's fourth husband, was humming to himself in the bathroom as he shaved. She saw that his hand tremor was a little worse tonight and he'd nicked himself. She finished applying her lipstick and glanced up at the western-style outfits she'd chosen for them.

"Herb, dear," Kate called out. "Don't forget that Lucy wants to dance with you tonight." Lucy was Kate's sister and a recent widow. Lucy and Walt had been married for forty years when he died. For the past few months, Lucy had been a wreck. She found some solace working in her flower garden, weeding and pruning away her troubles, but

Kate thought she was too isolated. She had Lucy over to the house every morning for breakfast and conversation.

"Honey, there are plenty of available men out there just waiting to be found," Kate had reassured Lucy one morning. "You won't be a widow for long if you get out there and meet people."

But her words had not made Lucy feel any better. Kate had introduced Lucy to several available and wealthy bachelors, all friends of Herbert's, but she just didn't seem interested.

"I'm not like you. I can't marry a man I don't love, Kate," Lucy said, boldly.

"Love is for kids and fools," Kate replied. "A woman your age needs companionship, security, and a square dance partner once a week!"

She knew what she was talking about. Why, she hadn't married for love since high school. True, her husbands all loved her and if she found love again, that would be wonderful. But she wasn't going to spend her life searching for a soulmate.

When Herbert came out of the shower, she noticed that his hair seemed thinner than the last time she'd checked. He wore a thick, white towel wrapped around his waist. Kate gave him a quick kiss on the cheek. "I adore you, Herbert," she told him. "You've been so good to me. We've had a good time together, haven't we?"

He smiled at her and patted her arm. "Yes, we have, Katie. If I died tonight, I'd die a happy man." He turned, pulled his well-pressed shirt off the hanger, and slipped it on.

Herbert, Lucy, Kate and the other square dancers had a lively evening of fun and exercise. Herbert danced at least once with every woman in the room, drinking fruit punch and making everyone laugh. Kate had never seen him so frisky.

"You're such a lucky woman," Lucy told her, as tears welled up in her eyes. "I really miss having a man to love me. It's so lonely, being a woman without a husband. It's not that Walt didn't leave me plenty of money. He did, but what I really want is to find love again."

"Lucy, you know you are welcome to spend time with me and Herbert whenever you want," Kate replied.

"But I'd feel like a third wheel. If you were single, things would be different," Lucy said.

"I don't have to be single for us to spend time together. Why don't we go to a movie or dinner by ourselves some time," Kate suggested, when they returned Lucy to her home.

During square dancing three weeks later, Herbert fell ill suddenly, suffering stomach cramps and convulsions. He was rushed to the hospital, but his condition remained a mystery and he died within a week. Kate was furious to learn that Herbert had spent all of his money during his lifetime and died deeply in debt. Herbert's children were shocked as well, but they were most puzzled about the circumstances surrounding his mysterious death. They decided to have his body exhumed. The medical examiner discovered that Herbert had been murdered.

Who and what killed Herbert?

CASE NUMBER

CASE NAME

STATUS

☐ CLOSED ☐ OPEN

SOLUTION

SEE PAGE 119

42 On the Run

Paula ran, hands pumping, feet pounding, as she stumbled over the uneven gravel shoulder of the country road. She'd forgotten her shoes. Her feet were bruised, bleeding, but she kept running. She gulped air, her heart thumping so loudly that she feared her pursuers might hear it. And she was so tired and hungry. She hadn't eaten since breakfast. Why were they after her? What had she done?

She'd glanced back only once, miles ago, and the black van was still there, too close, coming too fast. The driver was someone she'd seen before, but she couldn't remember where. She'd ducked into a driveway, down a dirt trail behind the house, and run along the fire trail. If she could only make it to Larsen's Country Store, just up the road, she could use the phone, call for help.

There. She saw Larsen's, right where she knew it would be. A few hundred feet more, she'd be at the pay phone outside, around the back of the building, where she couldn't be seen from the road. Her head hurt. She'd run out without her pills.

Paula picked up the receiver, punched in the number, and then her credit card to pay for the charges. Her sister answered on the second ring. "Lisa!" Paula said, breathless still. "You have to help me! They're after me again!"

Lisa sighed with relief. She'd been pacing for hours, worrying about Paula. "Where are you Paula? I'll come pick you up." Her tone was weary, but Paula didn't notice.

"I ran through a creek to lose them. My shoes came off, and I lost my glasses," she said. Paula's panic was too real to ignore.

"Okay, honey. I'll come. Where are you?" Lisa controlled her anger, but barely. How could professionals be so inept?

Where was she? Paula looked around wildly. She didn't know! A man came quickly around the corner of the building and grabbed her arm, "Hey! You can't be out here like this!"

When he grabbed her arm, she swung the telephone receiver, hard, and hit him in the temple with it. He dropped to the ground, unconscious. Blood streamed from his ear until his heart stopped pumping.

Paula stared in horror, then ran past a black van and two white cars, evaded a woman who tried to catch her, and slipped back into the woods.

The search for Paula ended two days later, when she was found deep in the woods, washing her clothes in a creek. Paula put up a fight and almost escaped capture, but she was arrested and charged with manslaughter in the death of the man at the telephone.

Who was chasing Paula?

CASE NUMBER

43

CASE NAME

The Man in the Gray Flannel Suit

STATUS

☐ CLOSED ☐ OPEN

SOLUTION

SEE PAGE 120

Kevin Casper was found dead after suffering a gunshot wound to the head. His body was discovered in the fishing boat that was tied to the dock behind his lakefront home. Kevin habitually fished each night and his home was so remote from others that no witnesses heard the gunshot.

The police swarmed around the yard, the dock, and the house. "Well, what do you think, Doc?" Detective Holmes asked Dr. McCoy, the medical examiner. McCoy ignored him for a while longer, checking this and that, mostly trying Holmes' patience. But Holmes refused to ask again.

Finally, the doctor said, "Looks like Casper placed this revolver to his right temple, holding the gun in his right hand, and pulled the trigger."

Holmes asked, "So you're thinking suicide?"

"Looks that way. I'll need the autopsy to be sure. Any other indicators of suicide that you're aware of?"

"Yeah. I guess he'd been passed over for a big promotion at work, his wife had found out about a long-term affair with another woman, and his daughter recently left her husband and moved back home with the kids," Holmes said, reciting the facts he'd written in his notebook while interviewing Mrs. Casper briefly before he walked down to the dock.

A youngish man wearing a grey flannel suit walked from the house and approached Detective Holmes. "Cary Granite," he said, holding out his hand. Holmes shook it, noting the firm grip and calloused fingers.

"You're the son-in-law, right?" Holmes said, remembering the name. "Tell me, do you think anyone would have a reason to kill Mr. Casper?" Holmes stood between Granite and the medical examiner, blocking Granite's view of the body.

"Who wouldn't?" Granite said, chuckling at his own wit, both hands now stuffed into the outside pockets of his jacket. He rocked back and forth on feet clad in the kind of loafers kids wore in the 1950s.

"You didn't like the guy, huh?"

"Not much to like. Kevin Casper was one of the biggest jerks that ever lived. I'd have killed him myself if I thought I could get away with it." Granite said, seriously.

"Where were you last night?"

"At a party with about fifty other people in the city. Feel free to check." Granite grinned again.

"How did you learn about Casper's death?" Holmes asked.

"I just arrived and the maid sent me down here to talk to you. She said Casper had been murdered. Somebody did the world a great service, I'd say," Granite replied.

Holmes looked long and hard at Granite before following up with some rapid-fire questioning. Granite's responses came back just as quickly:

"Mrs. Casper?"

"They fight like cats and dogs. Cops have been called for domestic disturbances five or ten times."

"The boss?"

"Casper hit him with a tire iron last week when they had a fight in a bar."

"His daughter?"

"She hated having to move back home with him and resented that he'd always sided with her ex-husband," Granite finished. "Yeah, too bad the old guy killed himself. Just like him, though, to take all the pleasure out of it for everyone else."

Holmes looked at Granite carefully and glanced down at his hands, still inside his jacket pockets. "Maybe so." Holmes gestured to one of the officers nearby. "Morty, take Mr. Granite downtown and test his hands for gunshot residue. Collect his clothes, too."

"What? What do you mean?" Granite sputtered.

Holmes told him, "You're under arrest for murder. You have the right to remain silent."

How did Detective Holmes know that Granite killed Casper?

44 Politically Incorrect

My husband has stopped breathing," Irene said to the dispatcher. The famous politician was found face up, his shirt partially opened, and his open jaw showing the early stages of rigor mortis when paramedics arrived in response to his wife's frantic emergency phone call.

When the medical examiner arrived at the scene, Detective Wilson said, "We're thinking this is a drug overdose, Doc. The guy was a known heroin user. Even the wife admits that he liked to 'chase the dragon.'"

One of the rookie cops lifted an eyebrow. Dr. Lester took it upon himself to explain the term: "He liked to inhale the vapors of heroin heated on a piece of foil. It's the most inefficient use of the drug because so much of it is wasted in the process."

Detective Wilson continued, "We found six balloons of Mexican black tar heroin in the bedside table along with a pill bottle of Xanax." Both knew Xanax could be used to help a drug user detox after a long drug binge.

"Well, let's see what the body tells us," Dr. Lester said. He pulled on a pair of latex gloves and as he observed, he dictated into a small digital recorder his initial findings. "A red area over the victim's upper lip." He opened the eyelids one at a time. "Petechial hemorrhages in both eyes."

"What?"

Dr. Lester held up his hand in the classic sign for patience and continued his observations. "Two small, reddish brown marks on the chest." He turned the body over. "Bruises on his back, small scrapes on both wrists contain the distinctive markings of wrist restraints."

"You're thinking robbery gone bad?"

Dr. Lester didn't respond. His examination continued for another half hour. When he finished, Detective Wilson asked, "Any preliminary decision on manner of death?"

"I'll need to wait for the tox screen," he said, referring to the blood tests that would reveal the level of drugs in the deceased's body. "Maybe accidental overdose or suicide. But I'm thinking homicide."

Why?

45 Disappearing Corpse

The house was too clean. That was the first thing Dr. Sims noticed. If a murder was committed here, there should have been a mess. The human body just isn't that easy to kill, especially without making a mess. "You're sure this is the place?"

Detective Trent nodded. "She worked in a pizza joint, delivering until midnight. She went out on a run to this address and was never seen again. The guy who lives here made the call and accepted the pizza. He's admitted that much."

The doctor nodded, hands clasped behind his back and walked through the house again. Every room smelled like bleach and pine-scented cleaners. No dust particles, or other trace evidence, had been found. The CSI team had taken apart the drains, vacuumed the entire house, and sprayed chemicals on the walls and other surfaces checking for blood residue. They'd found nothing.

From the finished basement, Dr. Sims called to Detective Trent and his partner. Two uniformed officers came along, too. When they reached the carpeted television room, they found Dr. Sims laying with his cheek on the floor. "Come down here. Feel the carpet."

Trent did as he was told. His partner and the two officers did the same. Each of them sat back on their heels and looked at each other. Finally, Trent said, "It's damp. He's cleaned this carpet recently."

Dr. Sims ran the flat of his palm over the carpet's plush surface. "Yes."

He sprayed the carpet with Orthotolodine. It turned blue, showing a trace amount of blood. "Get the CSIs back in here to pull the carpet up. I suspect we'll find what we're looking for underneath the padding."

When the padding was pulled up, the CSIs found a pool of blood.

"I think you can convict the man who ordered the pizza now," Dr. Sims told Trent.

"Even if DNA tests prove that this is the girl's blood, we'll never convict him of murder without a body," Trent said.

"I disagree," said Dr. Sims. "All I need is this puddle."

How would Dr. Sims prove that the homeowner was a murderer?

CASE NUMBER

46

CASE NAME

Remains of the Day

STATUS

☐ CLOSED   ☐ OPEN

SOLUTION

SEE PAGE 121

To Oliver, it seemed as though new houses sprung up in his neighborhood almost overnight. He'd moved out here to escape the city's sprawl, but others had followed him, people who seemed determined to turn the quiet community into another metropolis.

Why didn't they just stay in the city and leave us alone? he thought.

Oliver pulled his truck up in front of the latest home site he'd been asked to approve, parked behind the septic system installer's rig, and stepped outside. The sharp wind whipped around the bed of his truck. He pulled the front of his sweatshirt together and zipped it up to his chin. He lifted the hood over his ears and grabbed a pair of gloves. The septic was going in this afternoon. They'd need to know exactly where to put them both and he had to sign off on the location for the county health department and approve the permit first.

He'd barely closed the door to his truck when Hank strode up and grabbed Oliver's shoulder. "I'm glad you're here, Ollie. We've got a problem. Damnedest thing I've ever seen in twenty-six years of digging septics."

"What is it?" Oliver asked, tucking the clipboard under his arm and following Hank's long strides around to the back of the lot. There he saw a man on a backhoe and another man staring down into the hole they'd begun to dig.

"See for yourself," Hank said, pointing straight down.

Oliver looked down and saw the bones. They were obviously too big to be a dog's and they didn't look like they belonged to a cow. There would be no house on this spot for a while, of that he could be sure. He opened his cellphone and dialed: "Sheriff Bates, we got a body out here on the old Jensen place. It's just bones. Looks kind of small. Maybe a child or a young woman."

Hank shook his head and stuffed his hands into his pockets. "They'll never figure out who it is."

"Sure they will," Oliver told him.

How could they identify the remains?

CASE NUMBER

CASE NAME

STATUS

☐ CLOSED   ☐ OPEN

SOLUTION

SEE PAGE 121

47

Time Wounds All Heels

Mrs. Morton and Mrs. Cottle met once a week for coffee after their husbands had left for work. Usually, Mrs. Dennis came, too. But today, she'd called with regrets. Mr. Dennis had come down with the flu and she needed to stay home to take care of him.

"My eye," Mrs. Morton said, reaching for her third buttered scone. Rosie Cottle was such a good baker. Of course, that's probably why she weighed 250 pounds (113 kg). But there was nothing wrong with a bit of upholstery on a woman, Mr. Morton always said.

"What is it, Marion?" Rosie asked, titillated by the promise of juicy gossip. The neighborhood was so quiet with the children back in school after the long summer. Thank goodness the new television season had started. Otherwise, these weekly coffee klatches would be the only thing she had to look forward to.

"Did you see that new show last week? The one about the unsolved crimes?"

Rosie nodded, her mouth full of scone and strawberry jam. She loved all those crime shows and her husband liked them, too.

"Well, one of the criminals looked for all the world exactly like Ralph Dennis. Exactly like him."

"No! Really?" Rosie thought this was more exciting than the time she'd found a lost kitten in her backyard. That had gotten her picture in the paper. Imagine what would happen to Marion if she was right about Ralph Dennis. Why, she'd be famous!

Marion continued: "Sometime back in the 70s, this guy in California killed his mother, his wife and three children. Then he ran away, the coward. He's been gone thirty years." Marion sipped her coffee, refusing Rosie's offer of a fourth scone. She didn't want to spoil her lunch.

"So, I stopped by their house and dropped off some cookies," she continued, "just to get a chance to go undercover and ask Mr. Dennis a few questions. Nothing really came of it. He says he's never been to California. But I called the police anyway and this morning they came here, gathering information for a warrant. I guess they'll look at Ralph's clothes and things to see if they can find any of that trace evidence you hear about on them TV shows." Marion dabbed at the crumbs on her plate.

"How do they know what he'd look like now?" Rosie asked. "People change a lot in thirty years, you know." She thought of the slim waist she had in high school and her husband's full head of wavy dark hair, long gone down the bathroom sink.

"Well now they have some sort of 3-D model of what he'd look like. And I swear, its Ralph Dennis' spittin' image."

They finished their coffee in thoughtful silence and then bid each other adieu. The next day, Rosie got an excited phone call from Marion: "Guess what?" she said, half out of breath. "The police got a search warrant. They tore Ralph Dennis' house apart, and they found some Digger pine needle fragments in a soil sample they got from a pair of his shoes. They said it was a big lead."

"I don't get it," replied Rosie, utterly confused.

How did the pine needles help solve the case?

CASE NUMBER

48

CASE NAME

Movie
Madness

STATUS

☐ CLOSED   ☐ OPEN

SOLUTION

SEE PAGE 121

The trendy art film theater was almost deserted on Tuesday night. When Rob and Martha arrived, they flashed their membership card, picked up a latte, and climbed to the balcony seats, where they noticed a couple from their old apartment building looking for a seat in the same section. Until the movie started, they spent the time catching up on each other's lives. John joked that he was waiting to see which one of the women would cry first. "I'm going to keep an eye on you both," he said.

Rob laughed and stretched his legs over the wide aisle. Martha put her latte in the cup holder, then set her coat and her handbag on the seat between her and John. They settled into the comfortable chairs and watched intently, happily entertained by the subtitled Italian film *Never Again* nominated for best picture of the year. Martha got a little teary near the end.

When the film was over, John and his wife headed home. Rob and Martha dallied a bit while they discussed the plot intently. The concession stand had closed an hour previously and now the remaining personnel were waiting to leave. Rob and Martha grabbed their coats and left, with theatre personnel locking the doors behind them. They completed the short drive home and went to bed. Both had early appointments in the morning.

Martha rose at 5:30 in the morning, showered and dressed. Already late for her appointment, she grabbed her keys, slipped her feet into sandals, and reached for her purse which was usually on the table by the door. Only there was nothing on the table. She checked the car and couldn't find the purse there either. Martha and her husband searched all over, even calling the movie theater to see if she had left it behind, but nothing had turned up. In the end, all she could do was cancel and replace all of her identification and credit cards.

A year later, Martha and Rob were denied a loan. When they asked why, they were told they had unpaid debts totaling more than $200,000, several of which had been sent to collection.

What happened?

CASE NUMBER

CASE NAME

STATUS

☐ CLOSED   ☐ OPEN

SOLUTION

SEE PAGE 122

49

Beer Run

"Man, it's hot," Andrew said, wiping his brow with his already soaked T-shirt. He thrust the shovel into the ground and lifted the dirt. The muscles of his arms and shoulders ached with the effort. For most of the day, they'd been digging post holes for the new fence his cousin wanted to build.

Jerry walked over to the cooler, pulled out another couple of beers, and tossed one to Andrew. "Take a break," he suggested, putting the cold can to his forehead. Sweat streaked down his face.

Both men swallowed the beer thirstily, crushed the cans, and tossed them onto the small pile at the edge of the driveway. "Gimme another one," Andrew said, leaning on the shovel handle.

"Can't. All gone," Jerry said.

"No problem." Andrew dropped his shovel and strode toward the pickup truck. "I'll be right back."

He stepped into the front seat, settled himself, and backed out of the driveway. In the rearview mirror, he saw Jerry return to digging as he rounded the corner. He pushed the air conditioning up to full blast and aimed the blowers at his face.

Less than a mile down the road, he heard the siren. He looked up to see a police car, lights flashing, behind him. Andrew pulled over to the shoulder and waited for the young officer to approach.

Andrew rolled down the window. "What's up?"

"You've got a tail light out in the back," Officer Connor informed him, leaning back from the beer fumes that wafted out of the cab. "Have you been drinking?"

"Just a couple of beers. Working outside today. Hotter than Hades out there," Andrew replied.

Andrew submitted to the Breathalyzer test and was arrested for driving under the influence when he blew a .10, more than the legal limit of .08 percent. But at trial, his attorney successfully challenged the blood alcohol results and Andrew was found not guilty. On what basis did she challenge the results?

CASE NUMBER

50

CASE NAME

Love is Strange

STATUS

☐ CLOSED ☐ OPEN

SOLUTION

SEE PAGE 122

Mary's mouth was agape, revealing distinctly unappetizing half-chewed pork fried rice. "Alex is stalking you?" She swallowed her rice with a swig of green tea.

Jane nodded. "Last night, after my run. I was out of breath already. He came out of nowhere and grabbed me while I was trying to open my door."

"Right at the dorm? Here on campus?"

"Scared me half to death. Look." Jane pushed her shirt sleeve up with shaky fingers. Her long pale fingers and red nail beds contrasted sharply with the deep purple bruises on her arm.

"But we all consider you the perfect couple. Aren't you?" Mary stared into Jane's unhappy face, trying to understand.

"He's so obsessive." Jane pulled her sleeve down. Glassy tears settled in her eyes and she placed her hand on her chest. "My heart pounded so hard when I told Alex that I truly do love him. Maybe we were meant to be together someday. But I'm too young to settle down now. I'm only twenty!"

"Well, I could be wrong, but I think you need to stop having sex with him then." Mary grinned at her.

Jane's frown disappeared and she broke into a smile. "You think?"

Two nights later, Jane was found dead at her front door. The medical examiner on the scene observed no trauma to the body or obvious cause of death. When Mary reported that Alex had been obsessively stalking her friend, Alex was questioned and released.

Did Alex kill Jane?

CASE NUMBER

CASE NAME

STATUS

☐ CLOSED ☐ OPEN

SOLUTION

SEE PAGE 122

51

Love in the Afternoon

Nate opened the door and staggered back, blasted by a stench unlike anything he'd ever encountered. Unable to breathe, he flipped the switch to turn on the ceiling fan and rushed over to open a window. He covered his nose with his sleeve, inhaling and exhaling in shallow spurts.

The room looked like a hurricane had passed through. Not only was every piece of furniture upended, but newspapers were strewn about, plants were knocked over, and both of the glass doors that once enclosed the bookshelves were shattered. The carpet was soaking wet. But none of that explained the odor.

Nate walked into the kitchen where more havoc revealed itself. He saw Elaine's body laying face down on the tile floor. Her head had been bashed in and he saw right away what the murder weapon was: the small statue of Poseidon she'd bought in Greece last year. It lay near her left hand and was completely covered in blood. A pan of eggs congealed on the stove. She held a spatula in her right hand. From the smell, he could tell she'd been dead quite a while. He stuffed the note she'd sent him back into his pocket. Somehow, his affair and their fight were no longer important.

Later, the police detective questioned Nate out on the sidewalk in front of Elaine's apartment while the crime scene crew collected evidence inside.

"I came over because she'd sent me this letter a few days ago telling me she didn't love me anymore," he said. "She'd met someone new. She was very happy."

"So you killed her?" Detective Black asked.

"No! I mean, I was upset, of course. It hurt to read the letter, but I didn't kill her. I called several times and left a message saying I understood and we could still be friends," Nate replied. "When she didn't answer the phone for a couple of days, I decided to come and talk to her in person."

"Where's this letter?"

Nate pulled the note out of his pocket along with another paper and handed them both over.

"I had it analyzed," he said, indicating the analysis from Dr. Penn, a certified graphoanalyst. "She couldn't love me. She was incapable of love."

Detective Black watched Nate carefully, looking for signs that he was mentally unstable. He didn't appear to be crazy. Nate handed him a neatly folded letter. The first thing the detective noticed when he opened the letter was that the handwriting slanted hard to the left.

"When did you get this?"

"A few days ago, why?"

"I don't think your ex-girlfriend wrote this letter," said the Detective.

"What?" asked Nate, confused.

Why doesn't Detective Black believe that Elaine wrote the letter?

CASE NUMBER

52

CASE NAME

The Cutting Edge

STATUS

☐ CLOSED   ☐ OPEN

SOLUTION

SEE PAGE 123

His wife, Linda, had been stabbed to death and Arnie wasn't about to let the killer go unpunished. Arnie got right into Detective Ruby's face, his angry eyes staring into the man's professionally calm ones. "What do you mean you can't positively identify the knife? You and I both know that scum killed my Linda!"

Detective Ruby laid a hand on Arnie's shoulder. "Let's sit down a minute, and I'll go over what we've got."

Arnie didn't want to sit down. He wanted to hold onto his anger. But he also wanted to know the evidence. He sat. Ruby went to the coffee pot in the break room and brought back two cups of old, black sludge. Arnie took a big mouthful, burning his tongue. He swallowed anyway and didn't complain, waiting for Ruby to talk.

"We know your wife was alone in the office where she worked as a night courier. The fatal stabbing occurred just a few hours after her shift began. We think robbery was the motive, because money was stolen and another employee who sold jewelry at home parties had her desk jimmied open. Some jewelry was taken. We found one partial bloody fingerprint, but it's not complete enough for a conclusive match to our suspect."

Ruby stopped a second and sipped his own thick coffee. Arnie said nothing.

Detective Ruby continued, "We found cuts on her torso, her hands, and arms. There were some knife marks on the bone and in some of the cartilage in her hands. The fatal wound was directly to the heart, the medical examiner says. The knife marks were from a well-worn blade. And some of the wounds had a serrated edge."

"Yeah, and you found the cleaning guy and a knife in the trunk of his car. You arrested him! But you let him get off! How could you do that?" Arnie's patience had long ago expired. The wheels of justice ground too slowly for his taste.

"Let me show it to you," Ruby said, pulling an evidence bag containing a hunting knife from his desk drawer. Arnie looked at the knife's dull stainless steel handle, the long hand guard and the thin seven-inch blade.

"We think the knife we found is the murder weapon. It has Ed Morris' fingerprints all over it, but it doesn't have any blood or traces of her blood on it," Ruby explained, not liking the sound of it himself. "All the other evidence we've found is either inconclusive or exonerates him. I'm sorry."

Arnie put his head down on the table for a minute to think. It was hard to keep a clear head, but he knew he needed to do it for Linda. His wife deserved to have her killer brought to justice. Every day since her murder, his eyes had been glued to his computer screen, looking up information on anything and everything related to forensics, hoping for a way to get this guy. Suddenly, something occurred to him: "Tell me about the wounds again: Was there any bruising around them?"

"Actually, yes. There were some noticeable abrasions around the chest wound."

How could these abrasions help them prove the cleaning man's guilt?

Tourists basked in the pleasant temperature and the crisp fall sunshine as they waited at the base of Navy Pier, in Chicago. In just a few minutes, the tour boat filled, both upstairs and below deck. Young couples, families, and single men and women snuggled close together for the short ride up the Chicago River. There were even a couple of lap dogs on board.

Nancy took up the microphone and began the Architectural Tour on the Pride of Chicago. "After the great Chicago fire of 1871, which, by the way, was not started by Mrs. O'Leary's cow, architects flocked to Chicago, eager to be part of our city's rebirth. Today, we'll see more than thirty buildings that were, each in their own way, amazing examples of architecture at its finest. We're leaving from Navy Pier, first constructed in 1916, and renovated twice, in 1976 and from 1990-1994."

The boat passed Lake Point Tower, Aon Center, the NBC Tower, and moved north toward the River Cottages. While the boat turned around, the tourists could see a young couple being married along the river. The wedding photographer was taking rapid-fire shots of the couple with his digital camera, immortalizing the boat full of visitors forever.

Nancy said, "On the count of three, let's yell 'congratulations!' One, two three—" and before she could finish, a woman screamed from the deck below, followed by a large splash.

Joe, the security officer, ran quickly below deck and found a young woman, sobbing and holding onto a small Yorkshire Terrier as if the dog were essential to breathing. The dog wiggled, yapped, and tried to get away from her, but she was stronger. A man flailed in the cold water of the river. Joe tossed the man a life ring while the captain attempted to stop the ship. The woman cried, repeating, "He tried to steal my Tiffany." The man responded angrily, "She's a liar! Tiffany's my dog!"

Once the man was retrieved from the water, he and the woman and the dog were taken into police custody. Tiffany had a tag on her collar that listed her name, but no other information that could be compared to either tourist. Both tourists claimed that Tiffany belonged to them. None of the other passengers on the boat remembered which of the tourists had brought Tiffany on board. With all the commotion, the dog was nervous and unresponsive to both owners in question.

How did the security officer find out who was the rightful owner?

CASE NUMBER

CASE NAME

STATUS

54

Party
Animals

☐ CLOSED ☐ OPEN

SOLUTION

SEE PAGE 123

The party was in full swing when Calvin arrived at midnight. The music was so loud, he could hear it half a block from the driveway. He had to park that far away, too, and walk up to the house. As he approached, the sidewalk seemed to pulse with the vibrations from the sound system.

All the lights were on in the house, and Calvin was glad this place was so far back from the road. Built on a five-acre parcel, ten miles from Tampa, there were few neighbors to complain. He reached the front door, entered, and merged with the chaos.

Drake Newsome stood near the entryway with a beer in each hand: "Hey, Calvin! What took you so long, man?"

He gave Calvin a playful noogie and handed him one of the beers.

"All the ladies have been asking about you," he said.

Calvin rolled his eyes and stood with Drake for a minute, holding his plastic cup of beer and surveying the party guests. He could tell that Drake was at least five or six beers ahead of him.

"Hey man, watch out or you'll be an alcoholic before you turn seventeen!" Calvin joked, and set out to explore the rest of the mansion. He'd never seen so many rooms. Some were empty and others were packed with high schoolers smoking up and drinking to their heart's content. He drank another beer with a group of friends from the swim team and then wandered into a dark room upstairs.

Minutes later, Calvin bolted out the back door. The front of his shirt was drenched in blood. The sirens were getting louder as they got closer. He sprinted toward his Jeep as EMS workers ran by him, but he didn't make it much further before a young police officer spotted him. He pulled out his gun and told Calvin to freeze.

"What's going on back there?" Calvin asked, as if he had no idea.

"We got a call about a woman found dead in this house. Looks like you might have some information about that," he said, examining the blood on Calvin's shirt.

"I didn't do anything," Calvin said, his hands still raised above his head. The officer cuffed him and placed him in the back of the police car.

A thorough examination of the body and the crime scene revealed that a fifteen-year-old girl had been bound and gagged and stabbed to death. The weapon was nowhere to be found. They did, however, find a few hairs clutched in the victim's hand. Analysts compared the hair to a sample taken from Calvin and it was a match.

Did Calvin murder the girl?

CASE NUMBER

CASE NAME

STATUS

☐ CLOSED   ☐ OPEN

SOLUTION

SEE PAGE 124

55

Trouble in Paradise

Lucy and Harold lounged in the enormous bed, drinking mimosas and eating pastries. They'd arrived in the city two days ago and checked into the luxurious hotel last night for the first day of their honeymoon. So far, the experience had been idyllic. They couldn't believe their luck.

"Weren't those fabulous fireworks last night?" Harold asked, dribbling his mimosa into Lucy's gorgeously large navel and then bending down to lick it out.

She giggled when Harold's tongue tickled her midriff. "You mean before or after the, um, thing we did?"

Harold gave her a playful nibble. "You are bad! I mean the real fireworks. The ones out in the ocean."

Lucy grinned.

"Oh," she said, drawing the syllable out and giving it a suggestive twist. "Those fireworks. I'd never seen fireworks from bed before. It was pretty amazing."

"Well, we'd better get dressed and check out. Our cruise ship leaves from that very port out there in..." he said, stopping to glance at the clock on the bedside table, "two hours."

"And then we'll be cruising for two luscious weeks. How amazing is that!" Lucy said, applying a long, soulful kiss to his mouth that threatened to make them very late for check in on the ship. But neither one of them cared.

With a half-hour to spare, Harold finished up the video check out, struggling with their luggage as they ran to the elevator. Harold dropped the hotel key cards in the return box on the front desk, and they rushed to a waiting cab that whisked them off the departure dock. He didn't realize he'd forgotten his best sport coat until two days later.

When Harold and Lucy returned from their two-week idyllic honeymoon, they were shocked to find their bank account depleted, their credit cards maxed out, and a slew of messages from angry bill collectors on the answering machine.

The young couple were perplexed. They kept their credit cards and other personal belongings with them at all times.

How did Harold and Lucy get ripped off?

CASE NUMBER

CASE NAME

STATUS

☐ CLOSED   ☐ OPEN

SOLUTION

SEE PAGE 124

56

Highway to Heaven

Again and again, Richard slammed his palm onto the center of the steering wheel, forcing a long, loud blast of the horn to traverse the mere inches of space between his front bumper and the back of the slow sedan blocking his path. The old lady didn't get the hint. She just kept driving the speed limit, effectively preventing him from zooming toward the business lunch for which he was already much too late.

Richard was completely fed up with his commute and all the idiot drivers he had to deal with. He zoomed forward again, hoping to intimidate the old woman into pulling over and letting him pass. Just as he lifted his hand to honk the horn again, he saw a sudden flash of brake lights in front of him. His instinctive reaction was to veer around the car stopped in front of him, but that sent his SUV soaring off the two-lane road at forty miles per hour. The vehicle rolled over three times before coming to rest in a deep ditch off the side of the road. Richard wasn't wearing a seatbelt. While being tossed around in the vehicle, his neck snapped. He was pronounced dead at the scene. Amazingly, the vehicle was pretty much intact.

The old woman had continued driving until police stopped her on a local road about ten minutes after the accident. A jogger had seen most of the accident and was able to loosely identify the woman's Ford Taurus.

"Did you know that an accident occurred back there after you slammed on the brakes?" the officer asked, examining her vehicle.

Betty looked up at the officer with a confused expression.

"Oh, I'm sorry," she said. "I didn't know he was behind me. I saw an animal in the road, a little possum, and I had to stop and let it cross. I hope no one was hurt."

"A man was killed," explained the officer, surprised at how calm Betty was acting. "You're saying you slammed the brakes on to save a possum?"

"Yes sir," she answered, smiling sweetly.

Was Betty telling the truth?

CASE NUMBER

CASE NAME

STATUS

☐ CLOSED ☐ OPEN

SOLUTION

SEE PAGE 124

57

Stolen Glance

Ly Nguyen was working in her father's dry cleaner shop while he took a break for lunch. Mr. Nguyen had owned and operated his shop on the edge of town for twenty years, since he emigrated from his native Vietnam. Ly didn't work in the shop very often, but her father would trust no one else to handle the family fortunes. She tried to give him a rest from the backbreaking labor when she could leave her job at the library. Today was one of those days.

She stood behind the rack of freshly pressed shirts when she heard the bell indicating a customer had come into the front of the shop. At the same time, she heard her father enter from the door to his upstairs apartment.

"How can I help you, sir?" he asked. Ly had heard him ask the same question hundreds of times. But just now, he seemed a bit frightened. Ly walked around the shirts, carrying a batch of laundry tickets to be filed. When she glanced up, she saw a big Caucasian man dressed in a long coat holding a revolver pointed directly at her father, who was handing him the cash from the register. Ly gasped and stood frozen in shock. The thief heard her. He grabbed the cash, turned, and sprinted out the front door. A few seconds later, Mr. Nguyen crumpled to the floor. Ly hurried to her father.

"Father! Father!" she pled, but he seemed not to hear her. When another customer entered the store, she shouted to them, "Call 9-1-1!! My father's having a heart attack."

Police and paramedics responded quickly to the scene. While both Ly and Mr. Nguyen described the armed robber, their descriptions were inconsistent and the police were unable to locate a suspect. The only evidence left behind at the scene was a set of muddy shoe prints bearing the tread patterns of what appeared to be an athletic shoe.

A few months later, a tall, Caucasian man named Ned Lester committed an unarmed robbery at a convenience store in the same neighborhood. When the cashier refused to open the register, Lester ran out and was nabbed by police just a few blocks away. Shoe prints were found at that location as well, but the tread pattern was indicative of a dress shoe. A photo array lineup was presented to Mr. Nguyen and his daughter who could not positively identify Ned Lester as the man who robbed them. Lester himself swore that he had never set foot in the Nguyen's dry cleaner shop.

The officer in charge of the investigation was not convinced. He took another look at the shoe print evidence photographs and concluded, based on the ruler placed next to the shoe in both images, that both kinds of footwear happened to be the same size. Then he realized that there was another undeniable and unique similarity between the shoe prints from the first and second robbery.

What shoe print characteristic, aside from the tread print and shoe size, allowed the officer to identify Ned Lester as a repeat offender?

CASE NUMBER

58

CASE NAME

The Test of Time

STATUS

☐ CLOSED   ☐ OPEN

SOLUTION

SEE PAGE 125

Gilbert, pleased with his work, stood back to review and admire what he'd done. He'd worn two sets of latex gloves during the robbery, and he was unconcerned about leaving his fingerprints in the wrong places. But even if evidence of his presence was found, he wasn't worried. After all, he worked here. Of course, trace evidence would place him here, along with his seven coworkers, the cleaning crew, delivery service, and countless visitors. That's why his plan was so brilliant. And his execution had been flawless.

The Museum of Modern Detective Novels, normally a dusty old place of interest mostly to librarians like Gilbert, had become almost popular with the rise of the book collecting business. Gilbert realized that the museum's collection of rare books, including most of the popular commercial and literary fiction titles published in the past one hundred years, was a potential gold mine. Especially since security wasn't as tight as, say, a bank or a more prestigious museum might be.

He'd conceived the idea for the theft last spring when the Dashiell Hammett Estate announced the eightieth anniversary celebration of the publication of his groundbreaking novel, *The Maltese Falcon*. Gilbert realized an original signed first edition of the *Falcon* would bring almost as much money as the famed bird in the story itself. He couldn't suppress the smile that came from thinking about the fat fee he expected to collect.

Just for fun, in addition to the *Falcon,* he'd taken the museum's copies of *The Thin Man* and *Red Harvest*. They weren't as valuable as the *Falcon,* but the three titles made a nice set. Now, when the auction was finished, he'd be a wealthy man.

Looking over the display room once more, satisfied with the replacements he'd commissioned and substituted for the originals (he'd inspected each softly textured page himself), Gilbert turned out the lights, pulled the door closed, and locked it with his keys. He stripped the latex gloves off his hands once he reached the protection of his ancient Honda. A new car. Yes, that would be one of the first things Gilbert intended to buy. How wonderful.

Gilbert was genuinely surprised when the police showed up at his door a few days later. How was he caught?

CASE NUMBER

CASE NAME

STATUS

☐ CLOSED ☐ OPEN

SOLUTION

SEE PAGE 125

59 Crystal Clear

Mary Trails headed home from school after cheerleading practice at about 5 p.m. She was late and the cold winter brought nightfall too early. Her friend Jane was supposed to have given her a ride, but Jane had left a while ago and Mary had no other ride. The babysitter was supposed to leave at 5:30 and it was Mary's responsibility to watch her younger brother until her father came home from work. She began to run and decided on a shortcut through the woods. She had gotten lost that way once before. But she knew it would get her home faster, so she took the shortcut anyway.

It was early December and the ground was cold; a film of ice covered the earth. She slipped and fell twice. She wished she had worn slacks home from school, but she'd been in a hurry. Now her leg ached, but she ran deeper into the darkness.

Cindy paced the living room, dressed in her coat and hat, car keys in her hand, muttering with anger.

"Where are you, Mary?" she thought. "Can't you ever be on time? I could just kill you! I can't believe how irresponsible you are!"

Joey was in his room playing a video game. And Cindy needed to get home to care for her own kids. She considered leaving Joey alone until Mary returned, getting angrier by the minute.

At 9 p.m., Mr. Trails came home bearing fast food for dinner to find Cindy furious. "From now on, you will have to come home on time, Mr. Trails!"

Mr. Trails called Jane and some of Mary's other friends to find her. When no one knew where she was, he called the police. By 11 p.m., the police were searching the area for Mary. The trail in the woods yielded few clues. A few fibers from her cheerleading outfit were found, but Mary herself had totally disappeared.

The following December, a hunter found Mary's cold, dead body under a wool blanket about a half mile from one of the trails. The body looked to be in the early stages of decomposition. Apart from a few cuts on the right leg, there was no visible damage to the extremities or the body. As the police investigated, people in town began forming their own theories about Mary's disappearance. Some thought she had gotten lost that night a year ago and frozen to death. Others thought she'd been held captive in somebody's basement until recently escaping.

Then, the coroner found something curious: large ice crystals inside Mary's heart. The cause of death was ruled as suffocation.

Where had Mary been all this time?

60 Making Scents of It All

Speed dating? You've got to be kidding," Lori said. She wasn't interested in any more lame matchmaking programs. She'd been divorced for ten years and in all that time, she'd tried joining health clubs, church groups, shopping at the trendy market, bowling, and just about every other "meet-your-soul-mate" idea that had come her way. But sitting down in a big room with twenty other women, doing a five-minute speed date with twenty guys who couldn't even pick up a woman in a bar? No way.

"Oh, come on. It's not like you've got big plans for Wednesday night," Maggie coaxed.

"Yes, I do. I'm preparing for a colonoscopy!" Lori retorted and slammed the phone. Speed dating. The very concept was ridiculous. What could you learn in a five-minute date, anyway? Humiliating. She wouldn't do it. No. She wasn't that desperate.

But Maggie was. She called Lori on Thursday afternoon, when Lori had returned from her colonoscopy procedure and was still a little groggy from the sedation. "Guess what? I ran into an old flame at speed dating!"

"Who, Maggie?"

"Mr. Right! We're going out Saturday night. He's the one, Lori! I know he is!"

Lori groaned. Mr. Wrong, more than likely. Maggie had had a string of lousy boyfriends and she was attracted to men who didn't take long to reveal their true selves. There was Leo, who had beaten Maggie and, when she broke off their relationship, had stalked her until she got a restraining order against him. And Harry, the cocaine addict, who freaked out in Maggie's home and broke every piece of her mother's crystal. Oh, and then there was Rick, the mall security guard who stole for a living. Not to mention Joshua, the drummer who borrowed and never paid back all of Maggie's savings to keep the band alive, and Michael, the liar who was not only married, but also had another girlfriend.

Maggie had never been married and she claimed she could actually hear her biological clock ticking in the middle of the night. Lori had tried to explain that she was hearing her own blood pulsing in her ears, but Maggie said she was almost out of time: She was thirty. Lori scoffed.

"Okay, Maggie," she said. "Call me in the morning and tell me all about it."

Maggie didn't call Lori the next morning and didn't show up for work. By noon, Lori was really worried. She went to Maggie's house on her lunch hour, but Maggie wasn't home. Lori called the police department and reported Maggie missing. She gave the police the entire list of Maggie's jilted lovers.

Two days later, Maggie's partially clothed body was found in a ravine near her home. The coroner said she was killed by a double gunshot wound. Both bullets entered her body through the same hole and were still lodged in her chest. The bullets came from the same .38 caliber gun. But what was most peculiar was that her clothes smelled of black licorice.

Which of Maggie's past lovers was responsible for killing her?

CASE NUMBER

CASE NAME

STATUS

☐ CLOSED   ☐ OPEN

SOLUTION

SEE PAGE 126

61

One of a Kind

Glancing around to be sure Felix was nowhere nearby, Nadine waited in the dark rain for the door to open, then pulled her small car into the garage. She was afraid to leave the car, so she stayed inside with the car doors locked. Felix had been stalking Nadine for a month, since she refused to date him at the office holiday party. He lingered near her desk at work and followed her out of the office building on her way to lunch. Last week, he'd followed her home and parked on the street in front of her house for an hour. She applied for a restraining order against him, but the hearing wasn't scheduled for two weeks. Felix's behavior was creeping her out and she'd become afraid of her own shadow.

Hands shaking, Nadine called her brother. She'd explained the situation to him yesterday and he'd been furious, and protective.

Brian answered on the first ring. "Hey, sis, what's up?"

His easy camaraderie was just what she'd hoped for.

"I just got home. Would you stay on the line while I go inside and make sure everything is okay in my house?"

Nadine knew she sounded like a total idiot, afraid of the boogey man in the dark, but she couldn't help it. Brian didn't try to cajole her out of her fear.

"I'm about two minutes away. Just stay where you are and I'll be right over."

When Brian arrived, they entered her contemporary-style home through the door connecting the house to the garage. As soon as she stepped into the kitchen, the little hairs stood up on the back of Nadine's neck. "He's been here. I can feel it."

"Let's just look around," Brian said, confident as a big brother should be. He turned on the lights and began walking through the small house. After ten minutes of investigation, he froze near the glass-paneled bathroom door.

"Well, it's not a fingerprint, but they say no two are alike," he said after a long pause.

What clue made Brian believe that Felix had been inside the house?

62

Not My Type

☐ CLOSED ☐ OPEN

SEE PAGE 126

I'm a sucker," Dylan moaned, his head in his hands, elbows on the bar. He'd been sitting there, drinking straight whiskey for three hours. The words were slurred now, syllables indistinct.

"What's that, buddy?" Walt asked, willing to humor the guy now that the crowd had died down. "I can't understand you."

Walt shook his head, moving away from the stench of alcohol. No doubt about it, he was gonna need to call the guy a cab. Everything in Key West was within walking distance, to be sure, but no way could this dude walk outta here.

"I've been taking care of this boy since he was a baby—his mom swore that he was my kid and that she needed the help, so I helped her. I even got a little attached to him once I got used to the idea of being a daddy. Now that he's seventeen, my friend tells me she's been lying all these years and he's not really my boy!" Dylan said, holding up his empty glass. Walt filled it again. He took the change from the second hundred dollar bill Dylan had pulled out, which was still laying on the counter, to pay for the drink, and returned the remainder. By now, Walt wasn't expecting much of a tip. He figured Dylan was going to drink up the whole hundred, and then some.

Dylan swallowed the drink in one gulp. "Can you believe it? It's not even the money, it's the deception!"

"You know, you could have her arrested for extortion. But you better make sure first that it's not just a rumor," said Walt, trying to offer the guy some hope.

"You're right. He does look a lot like me, crooked nose and all. I'll get a blood type test tomorrow and find out if he's my kid."

Will the test confirm that Dylan is the boy's father?

CASE NUMBER

63

CASE NAME

Life Sentence

STATUS

☐ CLOSED ☐ OPEN

SOLUTION

SEE PAGE 126

Gregory was sick of the whole thing: Arlene's constant griping, her medicines, her snoring keeping him awake, and when she stopped breathing five or six times an hour, he couldn't sleep at all. Since she'd entered menopause, her asthma had gotten even worse. They'd been married for thirty-four years, longer than a life sentence for murder. He'd promised to love her until death, but he hadn't thought it would be his death from aggravation.

"Gregory! Are you out there?" Arlene called from the kitchen where she was, no doubt, still in her nightgown at three in the afternoon. .

He ignored her. His only peace and quiet came when he was in the garage and she left him to his woodworking. Lately, he had been doing more and more woodworking when she was home. He would leave the door to the house wide open while he worked, partly because he knew the noise from the saw drove her batty. She called three more times, each progressively louder and whinier.

Gregory was tired of having to come running every time she needed him. He hoped that soon he would be free of her torment. A few minutes later, he put the sandpaper he was using down on the workbench and stood back to admire the rocking chair he was refinishing. He dusted his hands on his jeans and smiled at the amount of sawdust on the floor.

"I'm coming, I'm coming," Gregory murmured as he headed inside, nearly tripping over the fan he had placed in the doorway. Man, he was sick of this! If he'd known what a pain she was going to turn into, he'd never have married her. What had he been thinking?

Gregory entered the house, slipped off his shoes and his jacket and hung them on the hook by the door. "What is it, Arlene? What do you want?"

But Arlene didn't answer. Gregory found her lying on the floor, her skin bluish in color.

How did Arlene die?

CASE NUMBER

64

CASE NAME

Falling for Her

STATUS

CLOSED ☐   OPEN ☐

SOLUTION

SEE PAGE 127

The Yosemite Health Hikers stood around in the cool morning air, sipping coffee and chatting quietly. The breathtaking beauty that surrounded them demanded reverence, not loud banter. At least, that's what Shelly thought. Or maybe they were all sleepy. If Brandon didn't arrive soon, they'd leave without him.

"Hey, man! Where you been?" Taylor asked, holding a palm out for Brandon to slap as he approached.

Brandon dipped his head. "Had a late night." The other guys made suggestive noises implying a woman had been involved. "Okay, okay," Brandon said. "Let's go."

The group headed out on Yosemite Falls Trail toward their ultimate destination, El Capitan. They'd get there eventually. No one was in a hurry. Shelly refused to let Brandon spoil this hike. He had always been a jerk, even when they were dating. No reason to think he'd suddenly change.

They fell into step, Brandon and Shelly at the tail end of the group.

"Why don't you like me?" he asked her, as if he didn't know. He reeked of alcohol.

She rubbed her arm, reflexively, where he'd left a bruise the night she'd refused to have sex with him. He pulled a flask out of his pocket and added a splash of whiskey to his coffee. He offered the flask to Shelly and put it back into his pocket when she refused.

She sped up. "It's not that I don't like you..." she told him as he hustled to keep up. She actually despised him but wasn't sure how to tell him without getting into a big discussion. By now, they were at the base of Upper Yosemite Fall.

He wasn't fooled.

"If there's one thing I can always tell, it's when a chick doesn't like me. I've had lots of practice recognizing the cold shoulder," Brandon said, smiling.

Moments later, the other hikers turned to see Shelly running towards them, waving her hands frantically.

"Brandon fell!" she hollered. "Help!"

Two ominous pairs of footprints faced out over the precipice. Brandon's body lay forty feet below, ten feet from the base of the waterfall. Investigators found his flask teetering on the edge. Brandon had hit his head three times on the way down and his neck was bent at an impossible angle. The National Park Service's search and rescue team responded by helicopter and concluded that Brandon suffered a fatal head injury.

When Shelly was interviewed, she told investigators that Brandon had been drinking heavily.

"He seemed a little woozy," she said, "but I didn't notice that he had backed up too close to the edge. I cried out to him, but it was too late."

She started to cry.

Was Shelly at fault?

CASE NUMBER

CASE NAME

STATUS

65

Digging Up the Past

☐ CLOSED   ☐ OPEN

SOLUTION

SEE PAGE 127

I'm sorry there wasn't anything we could do with this," said Officer Bones. "There were no fingerprints on the letter or the envelope."

"What about saliva under the flap or the stamp to get a test sample for DNA analysis?" Sandy asked. There had to be a way to find this guy and get more information out of him.

"Unfortunately, our techs say no," he told her gently.

Sandy accepted the letter from him. "Tell me again about the circumstances surrounding his death," Officer Bones asked. "I might have missed something."

"When I was nine years old, my father took off to go fishing. He called it his 'alone time.' When he didn't return by afternoon, my mother got worried. She took me down to the lake where he normally fished, but we couldn't see any sign of him or his boat. I remember wading up to my knees in the frigid water, yelling his name. A few days later, rescue workers called off the search. We never saw my father again."

Getting the letter after all these years forced her to relive the most difficult part of her life. She had tried to let her father's memory go, despite the unanswered questions. Now those questions were beginning to torture her all over again.

Officer Bones read the letter aloud one more time:

Dear Sandy,

I have been meaning to write this letter for many years, but it took me until now to find the courage. I was only a kid when my brother and I found your father's body floating in the lake. We had been playing in the woods a day or two after he went missing and there it was. We were horrified. We didn't know what to do. My brother, who was a year older, decided that we would get in trouble if we told anyone. He said the police would think we killed the man. So we dragged him out of the water and covered him in leaves and dirt so no one would find him. I've kept this horrible secret for years, but I can't keep you in the dark any longer. You deserve to know the truth about your father. Maybe now it can help you grieve.

There was no signature or return address, but the remainder of the letter described where the body was left.

Officer Bones folded the letter and sat with it for a few moments. When he eventually spoke, he said: "I'm afraid this man is a phony."

How did he know?

THE SOLUTIONS

01 Short on Evidence

In 1985, English scientists discovered that each human has unique DNA, with the exception of identical twins. It wasn't until 1992 that the National Research Council backed DNA testing as a reliable method to identify criminal suspects. After that, the technology made its grand entrance into the mainstream court system. Fifteen years ago, when Shine was convicted, the prosecution in most cases was not doing routine DNA testing because the testing was cost prohibitive for most law enforcement budgets. In this case, the shorts the deceased was wearing when she was bitten could be examined for saliva, which would likely be present. Even after the passage of time, the saliva can be processed and DNA compared to Shine's. If it doesn't match, he'd be released from prison. If the DNA did match, his claims of innocence would be diminished, but not extinguished. After all, it wasn't the bite that killed the waitress. She was stabbed to death.

02 Good Neighbors

Edna Mae could see the form of Harry's body and the shape of a man standing over him, but no more. Her glasses were fogged over because she entered the warm house from the sharp cold outside. Her heavy breathing and the warm pie added to the humidity, making the fog heavier. Not only was she unable to see Harry's attacker, she was unable to see anything distinctly until her glasses cleared.

03 Double Feature

The audience could not distinguish the twins from each other, so no positive eye witness identification exists. Both brothers handled the murder weapon, so fingerprint evidence would not identify the killer. The blood of both sisters was also on the knife. Individually, each brother was drenched in the blood of only one of the sisters, but the evidence would not determine which sister bled on which brother. The DNA of identical twins is also identical. Thus, the DNA evidence could not distinguish which twin killed which victim or which one fathered the child. All the brothers had to do was to refuse to testify against each other, and they would both go free.

04 Food for Thought

While the surveillance cameras were not recording information, they did allow the stock clerk in the back room to watch the crime as it occurred. He was able to describe the unmasked killer in detail. The killer did get caught, but not as quickly as Evelyn had hoped. The bullet removed from Jake's body matched a bullet found at the scene of another nearby robbery. Police apprehended the man with the aid of the clerk's description.

05 Clean Sweep

No. If Theresa had fallen into the pool before Chad arrived at 3 p.m., her submerged cellphone (which the police found on her body) would have stopped functioning and voicemail would have picked up immediately when Emelda called at 3:15. But Emelda heard the phone ring a few times before voicemail kicked in, which meant that the phone was still on at 3:15 p.m. and Theresa was still alive when Chad arrived. Police would soon discover that Mrs. Fernandez had paid Chad a hefty sum to scare Theresa out of sleeping with her husband, but Chad had shown his usual lack of restraint and shoved the poor woman into the pool without knowing that she couldn't swim. Mrs. Fernandez came home to find that her plan had gotten way out of hand.

06 Love Crazy

Her motive was to find the stranger. Psychopaths are believed to be remorseless predators who use any means necessary to achieve their ends and to avoid detection. They are unable to distinguish right from wrong and feel no empathy toward others. This particular psychopath met a man and became attracted to him at her mother's funeral. Afterward, through a diligent search, she'd been unable to find him. She killed her father in the hope that the handsome stranger might show up at her father's funeral. She showed no regard for human life nor for her father's loved ones.

07 False Impression

Repeating the serial number was the first mistake Mr. Hudson had made as an inexperienced counterfeiter and for that, he'd already served his time. When the chauffeur saw the image of Abraham Lincoln on the doorman's $50 tip, he knew that Mr. Hudson was up to his old tricks again. Lincoln is pictured on the $5 bill. Ulysses S. Grant is pictured on the $50 bill. Mr. Hudson used a real $5 bill to forge a $50 bill and while the doorman fell for it, it wouldn't be long before someone else realized and traced the counterfeit money back to Mr. Hudson.

08 Little Footprints

Yes. Brenda couldn't have killed herself by falling on the pig, because there were only two pointy pig ears and six lacerations. Someone had killed her using the doorstop as a weapon. The footprints in her blood weren't Eric's, since he was wearing shoes. They weren't Brenda's, because her feet were bare and white. Kelly had grabbed the doorstop on her way in the house and made the phone call to lure her mother inside. When Brenda entered the foyer, Kelly swung the heavy doorstop, stunning her mother. A second hit and then a third knocked Brenda to the floor unconscious and left six deep lacerations on Brenda's scalp. Left untreated, Brenda bled to death while Eric was passed out poolside. Those were Kelly's footprints in her mother's blood.

09 Smoke Signals

It occurred to Bill that if smoke inhalation were the cause of death, the canary would have died of it long before its owner. Birds are particularly susceptible to the inhalation of smoke, and they may die when exposed to relatively small amounts of fumes. That is why canaries were used by miners to detect the presence of pockets of gas underground—the birds would die when exposed to the slightest amount of gas and long before the miners noticed it. Because the bird was inside the man's bedroom and was unharmed, and because the body was not burned, it seemed more likely that the old man was dead before the fire started.

Police later discovered that the old man's wife had met someone with an even bigger home and wallet. She killed her husband to cash in on his life insurance, and set fire to the place to cover up the crime.

10 Hanging by a Thread

Most cheap uniforms are made of 100 percent polyester. Jennifer's ex-husband wore a polyester postal worker's uniform, but that wouldn't account for the strange shoe print found in Jennifer's kitchen. The fiber actually came from a baseball uniform, and the strange shoe print was left by a baseball cleat. The opposing baseball team almost had to forfeit the game because they were one player short at first: Their pitcher, George Wilson, showed up twenty minutes late to the game. George had eventually arrived wearing his polyester baseball uniform and cleats, the ones that formed the unique pattern on Jennifer's kitchen floor. Arriving late would have given him enough time to get in and out of Jennifer's house before she arrived home from work. When brought in for questioning, George quickly broke down and admitted that he had burglarized Jennifer's home to steal her son's lucky baseball glove. When he was unable to find it, he grabbed some other items to make the trip worthwhile.

11 Big Crime on Campus

Dental enamel is the hardest substance in the human body and is often used to assist in identification. A forensic dentist can identify unknown perpetrators by matching dental patterns with dental impressions left on relatively hard surfaces, such as cheese or apples. Students are likely to have dental records on file with the college's health services. All the police have to do is compare the dental impressions in the food with the college dental records. If one partying student is located, it is likely others will be identified, too. A week later, local police arrested a twenty-one-year-old student and three of his fraternity brothers for the crime. All four were flunking Veronica's class and had taken revenge in the way that came most natural to them.

12 Heir Apparent

Yes. Despite her doubts, Olivia could find out by comparing her maternal mitochondrial DNA with Harvey's. Maternal mitochondrial DNA is inherited and unchanged along maternal lines for many centuries. It is very hard, survives for long periods of time in decayed and skeletal remains, and is found in all body cells, the teeth pulp, and even in hair shafts, which don't contain normal DNA. If Nana and the famous actress were related through their mothers, then the mtDNA obtained from the hair shafts of their descendants (female or male, alive or dead) can be compared. After some convincing, Olivia managed to get a hair sample from Harvey and had it compared to her own. They were a match: Virginia Haynes and Olivia were first cousins, twice removed.

13 Gambling Man

Officer Clark was wrong. Native Americans can have eyes of any color. It is a myth that Native Americans "normally" have brown eyes, or that two brown-eyed parents only produce brown-eyed children. It depends on the actual ancestry and the eye color of the ancestors of the particular person in question. With the racial intermixing that has occurred over the past several hundred years, eye color of human offspring can be almost anything. Only genetic research and DNA testing can answer the question of ancestry. If the serial killer's motive was to weed out the imposters, then he hurt his cause by killing one of his own people.

14 Cold Comfort

All forensic science is based on the Locard Exchange Principle which states that every contact one makes with another person, place, or thing results in a physical exchange of material. Sometimes, these materials are microscopically small trace evidence. But in this case, police found clearly visible white hairs. There are three basic types of scale patterns found on the cuticle, the outer layer of a hair shaft: While impricate, or flattened, scales are found in humans, coronal, or mosaic-like, scales are common in rodents and spinous, or triangular-shaped, scales are more typical of cats. When police saw that the white hair featured spinous scales, they knew that it was most likely a cat hair and not a human hair. They were then able to match the hair to that of an orphan cat housed at the local animal shelter where Louise's paperboy volunteered. The paperboy confessed when police found Louise's heirlooms in a shoe box under his bed.

15 Shocking Evidence

When someone, such as Mr. Edwards, donates their organs, their eyes and several other organs are harvested by a local organ bank soon after death. But what June remembered was that organ banks also keep blood samples and frozen blood serum from all donors in case they are needed by the organ recipient in the future. Thus, she could obtain Mr. Edwards' blood from the organ bank, have it retested using all the correct procedures, and obtain admissible evidence to prove he was intoxicated.

16 Intoxicating Question

Because he had lost a game of pool. It would be uncharacteristic, though not impossible, for a local pool champion to lose a game of pool unless he was very drunk. Depending on who the guy was playing, the lawyer was hoping to use this to his advantage. If the bartenders had a clear view of the pool table, as he/she probably would in a tiny bar, they would have witnessed a difference in his motor skills, reaction time, and judgment, which could qualify as visible evidence of his intoxication level.

17 Sharp Reality

A piece of glass from the broken vodka bottle. Most knife stab wounds are deeper than they are wide. Logan's chest wound was inconsistent with the blade of a pocketknife. When Bud charged at Logan, both Logan and the vodka bottle were knocked to the ground. Logan sustained the wound by rolling onto a big, jagged shard of broken glass on the floor. The tip of the glass shard broke off in his chest as he rolled.

18 Where There's a Will

Because the letter was written three years ago, before Dr. Hindricks' stroke, it could not prove that the will was a forgery. Handwriting can change considerably after a debilitating illness, thus a difference in handwriting between the letter of recommendation and the will would not necessarily indicate a forgery. A handwriting expert would need comparison samples from after the stroke to truly assess whether the overall form, line features, margins, and format were consistent with the handwritten will. Whether the will was a forgery might have remained a mystery if the nephew hadn't heard that Melissa's husband had been falling short on his child support payments and had recently skipped town without leaving a forwarding address. In a moment of weakness, Melissa confessed to forging the will to make up for the missing income. The lawyer, taken in by her beauty, was a willing accomplice.

19 Black and Blues

Bruises, or contusions, like Susan's are caused by tiny blood vessels broken by a blow. A bruise darkens to purple in the first few days, then fades for about four or five days before turning green, brown and finally yellow. If Susan had bruised herself on Tuesday as she said, the bruise would have passed the purple stage by Sunday. She had to have been hit within the past few days and David, who had hit her before, was the most likely offender.

20 The Convenient Thief

No. Mr. Alfred never mentioned what was stolen. While Mr. Alfred may need more evidence to press criminal charges, Philip couldn't have known that junk food was stolen unless he took it himself or watched his friends take it. Body language can also indicate that someone is lying. Along with the usual signs of nervousness, lack of eye contact, sweating, and so on, detectives also look for small gestures like a wrinkling of the nose, a downward curl in the corners of the mouth, touching of the face, throat, or mouth. Touching or scratching the nose, or behind the ear, is also highly suspect.

21 Twin Terrors

While identical twins do have identical DNA, fingerprints are individual. No two people share identical fingerprints. Despite the eyewitnesses' inability to distinguish one twin from the other, the authorities were able to use the fingerprints on the beer bottle to identify which of the twins yielded the murder weapon.

22 Dead Man Gawking

Regardless of the wound, blood clots within minutes of leaving the body. When blood oozed out of the victim's mouth, the gawker knew that he couldn't be dead because dead men don't bleed. At death, the heart stops pumping and blood no longer circulates.

---

23 The Long Goodbye

Jenny had found an unexpected murder weapon that appealed to her girlish senses: nail polish remover. She had read in the library that some nail polish removers contain cyanide, so she picked up a bottle at the drug store that night, used it on her nails, and then added a little bit to Max's evening medication. Because cyanide poisoning is rare, it is generally not suspected, particularly in a death attended by the family. The symptoms mimic senility and aging or cardiovascular disease, and cardiac arrest is usually the end result of both. Cyanide is a colorless gas with a faint, bitter, almond-like odor. Nearly 40 percent of the population is unable to smell cyanide at all because they lack the necessary gene for detecting the odor. Fortunately for Max's kids, who wanted to know the truth, the medical examiner was among the other 60 percent.

---

24 Breathing Lessons

The excessive soot and carbon monoxide found in their bodies indicates death by smoke inhalation. When a building burns, smoke and other noxious gases fill the building from the top down. This is why smoke detectors are placed on or near ceilings. When Manny and Corrine heard the fire alarm in the middle of the night, they must have sat up in bed, stood up, and attempted to walk or run outside. Had they been crawling when they were overcome by the smoke, their bodies wouldn't have been found lying flat on the floor but rather in some form of bent knee position. It took only a few breaths to drop them in their tracks. Instead, they should have rolled off the bed onto the floor, where the air was likely to be less toxic, and then crawled to safety.

25 Where's Waldo?

Waldo allegedly drowned in an inland lake, which would mean there was nowhere for his body to go and yet the body still hadn't been found a year later. He also had a mistress, which might have given him motive to fake his own death to avoid a messy, costly divorce. But the real kicker was the robbery: Elmer couldn't help but think that Waldo had hired someone to "steal" his assets so he could take them with him in "the afterlife." Then Waldo would have disappeared, moving far away with his mistress. Elmer's theory was correct. Waldo had spent the past year paying cash for everything and creating a whole new identity for himself.

26 Helping Husband

Initially, the medical examiner thought Nettie died of a cerebral aneurysm or a bulge in a blood vessel of the brain. Her symptom of a strong, persistent headache was the warning. Nettie smoked, and smoking increases the risk of cerebral aneurysm. But the autopsy revealed a significant overdose of Tagamet. The final dose not quite dissolved in the stomach contents must have been in the tea Joe Sr. served her. Tagamet is used to treat stomach ulcers, excessive amounts cause diarrhea, headache, fatigue, dizziness, muscle pain, rash, confusion, low blood pressure, and renal failure in fifteen to thirty minutes.

27 Hard-Hearted Woman

Both Mickey and Marianne contributed to Steve's demise, although neither one intended to kill him. Steve died from a sudden cardiac death caused by two chest wall blows coming close together. Fundamentally, it's a bad idea to strike the chest. Two such blows in a short period of time were too much for Steve's heart to withstand.

28 Strip Tease

When Ellie's purse tumbled to the floor, handcuffs had spilled out. When Roger saw the cuffs, he knew that she was either a naughty hooker or a cop, so he played it safe and pretended he had only called for a massage. Ellie was in fact an undercover cop who had blown her cover.

29 Isolated Incident

Old Tommy was struck by lightening during the storm. Old Tommy made the mistake of being near his clothesline, probably holding the wires when he was struck. The red fernlike marks on his back, called Lichtenberg figures, are named after a German physicist who discovered them in 1777. While they don't always occur, when present they are clear evidence of a lightning strike.

30 All in the Family

Ace knew that his father was allergic to latex and remembered that Doctor Bandit wore latex gloves as part of his costume. People who are allergic to latex gloves get bumps, sores, cracks or red, raised areas on their hands twelve to thirty-six hours after wearing them. It had been eighteen hours since the robbery when Ace walked into his father's house. Mr. Morris confessed and told Ace that he had bought the surgeon apparel online.

31 Bubba's Fresh Fish

Alligators kill large prey by dragging it underwater, drowning it, tearing it into large pieces and then swallowing it. Because the arm was smoothly severed and not torn, it had to have been amputated by a knife or some other sharp instrument, not by an alligator's teeth. Also, if Bubba was fishing for grouper, he must have been fishing in salt water (grouper is a saltwater fish). Alligators are not found in saltwater.

32 Dumbfounded

Maggie had become extremely dehydrated in the Arizona heat. Extreme dryness of her nasal membranes had resulted in crusting, cracking, and bleeding from the nose, which explained the dried blood on her face. After ruling out signs of foul play on autopsy, the medical examiner concluded that Maggie died from heat stroke caused by the exposure to extreme heat and complicated by her obesity and alcoholism.

33 The Look of Death

Jane Doe was shot to death. A significant gunshot wound is the only cause of death that would be visibly obvious to Doug, an untrained observer, on a nude body that has spent at least three weeks in the cold water. Even submerged in cold water, the hands and face are swollen, parts of the skin are separated from the body, and fingernails would be lost. The bullet hole in her forehead would still be visible because it had to have penetrated the bony skull to kill her.

34 Guy Trouble

No. If Zack had shot himself, he would have immediately dropped the gun, and it would have been found near his body with the other evidence the crime scene tech removed. Zack was murdered. Police were able to lift a fingerprint off the candy wrapper that dropped from the killer's pocket when he left the scene of the crime. Zack's neighbor was arrested for murder.

35 Small Town Secrets

No. Although influenza was one of the leading causes of death at that time, it hadn't killed Mrs. Wilson. In 1905, marijuana, heroin, and morphine were all available over the counter at corner drug stores. The fact that heroin was regarded as safe and effective for treating stomach and bowel trouble made it easy for the doctor to use it as a murder weapon. Mrs. Wilson's symptoms of stomach spasms and constipation, bluish colored fingernails, drowsiness, and loss of breath are classic signs of heroin overdose. Now, Dr. Wilson is free to marry Miss Button.

36 Drowning in Mystery

No one. Mr. Larson and his wife faked his death to collect on his life insurance. They operated on the belief that crimes at sea are rarely reported and even more rarely investigated and solved. Unfortunately for them, the captain realized that Mrs. Larson could not have been diabetic if people had witnessed her drinking that much alcohol. A diabetic would have fallen into a coma and probably died from consuming as much as she had. So what was in the cooler? Since no human can survive a loss of four liters of blood, Mr. Larson had drawn his own blood over time, froze it, and brought it onboard with him in the cooler they claimed contained Mrs. Larson's insulin. Then they used that blood as murder "evidence." Mr. Larson was still alive. He was lying low in disguise, waiting to sneak off the ship at the next port.

37 Ill Will

Hair analysis is not just useful for confirming exposure to certain drugs, it can also provide a timeline of that exposure. As hair grows, the follicle cells undergo changes that manifest themselves in the growing hair shaft. Because it's known that hair grows about half an inch per month, toxicologists can "read" a strand of hair from end to root like a timeline. In this way, experts can determine Mrs. Cash's exposure to morphine over time to determine whether she truly was addicted. A thorough analysis of Mrs. Cash's hair proved that she was not a morphine abuser. After hours of interrogation, Dr. Charity confessed to injecting Mrs. Cash and several other patients with an overdose of morphine. He then forged her signature on the will to claim all her money. As for the medical records that seemed to back up the doctor's story: Dr. Charity made those entries after his victims died, and predated them. On a computer, such adjustments are easy to accomplish. But he forgot that the medical practice computer was equipped with an internal clock that verified the exact dates and times the entries were actually made. A pattern of deception was easily proven.

38 Bone of Contention

No. He suspected that the guilty party was someone to whom John had donated his bone marrow—most likely a relative with a blood disease. DNA samples from transplant recipients contain a mixture of their own DNA and that of the donor's. John Orr could not have committed the crime from jail, but he could have previously donated his bone marrow to the real perpetrator, thus giving the perpetrator his DNA. The police checked hospital records and found that Orr had donated bone marrow to his brother three years prior. Orr's brother was Judy's assailant. The fingerprint evidence in this case was more reliable than the DNA evidence.

39 Sticky Situation

No. Palm prints are not kept in the various databases where finger prints are stored. Criminals are not routinely palm printed upon arrest and the jobs that require finger-prints, bonding, and licensing do not also require palm prints. If a suspect is located by police investigation, his palm print could be taken and positively identified by compari-son, but a palm print alone, no matter how unusual, won't help police identify a suspect.

40 Death Hits a Dinger

No. The medical examiner testified that the broken forearms were defensive wounds. They indicated that Lefty had attempted to defend himself from the attack. So he wasn't dead after the first blow, as Jack claimed, and the murder was not self defense.

41 For Love or Money

Herbert died of chronic arsenic poisoning, made evident by hair analysis performed by the toxicologist. Arsenic is deposited in the cells of the hair follicles in proportion to the amount of arsenic in the blood when the cell was produced. It was clear from Herbert's hair follicles that he had been given small doses of the poison over an extended period of time. The hand tremors while shaving and the hair loss were both symptoms of the poisoning. The suspect list for a chronic poisoning would include only those with long-term contact with the victim, such as family members. Herbert's sister-in-law, Lucy, had visited the Black household every morning for the past few months, which gave her opportunity to slip a little poison into Herbert's coffee. She hadn't killed him for the money. She had only wanted Kate's companionship, and Herbert stood in the way of that. The arsenic that killed Herbert was found in Lucy's gardening shed, in a weed killer she used in her flower gardens.

42 On the Run

The people chasing Paula were workers from the group home where she lived as a paranoid schizophrenic patient. The woman she evaded in Larsen's parking lot and the man she killed with the phone were not trying to harm her; they were trying to bring her back to the group home from which she had escaped earlier that day. Paula didn't recognize them because she had dropped her glasses in the creek and because she was in a state of panic. Her sister, Lisa, was distraught on the phone because the professionals hired to keep her sister safe had allowed her to escape.

43 The Man in the Grey Flannel Suit

Granite had just arrived at the scene and had no information about Casper's death except the maid's story that Casper had been murdered. Granite couldn't see Casper's body and wasn't present when Dr. McCoy told Holmes that Casper had committed suicide. The only way Granite would know that is if he had seen the body previously, which, according to his alibi, he hadn't.

44 Politically Incorrect

The victim's body shows signs of death by "burking." The term "burking" dates back to 1829, when a heavyset murderer named William Burke was hanged in Edinburgh after his cohort Edward Hare admitted that Burke sat on their victims while Hare suffocated them, and the pair sold the bodies to medical schools. The red area around the politician's upper lip was probably caused by compression as his mouth rubbed against something like a towel or pillow. Bruises on his back and the two marks on his chest suggest someone leaning on his body to prevent his lungs from expanding to take in air. Petechial hemorrhaging, or burst capillaries, is a condition generally caused by strangulation or asphyxiation.

45 Disappearing Corpse

Dr. Sims was able to confirm that the blood belonged to the pizza girl by DNA tests. He then estimated the volume of blood in the victim's body by her size. Because the CSIs found 2000 cc of the victim's blood under the carpet, Dr. Sims testified that if she'd lost that much blood, she had to be dead. The jury agreed, although no body was found.

46 Remains of the Day

If the bones Hank found are really those of an adolescent, then it will be easier to determine the decedent's age: Bones and teeth in children follow a fairly predictable growth pattern and could help authorities pinpoint the age more easily. Determining sex from a child's skeletal remains is often more challenging, since gender-specific identifiers don't appear until after puberty. In this particular case, the forensic anthropologists will first gather as much information as possible from the appearance of the bones. Based on the profile they create, DNA samples will then be taken from the bones and compared to parents of potential victims matching that profile.

47 Time Wounds All Heels

Plant materials can be very useful to forensics experts. Because some plants are native to specific locations, they can sometimes help link a suspect to the crime scene. In Ralph Dennis' case, the crime scene was in California, where the suspect said he had never been. The specific type of pine needle found in the soil sample of his shoes was a Digger pine needle, native to the state of California. They grow only at low elevations in the Sierra Nevada and in the coastal ranges of California, thus Mr. Dennis had to have lied about never visiting California. Analysts proved that Mr. Dennis had lied when they were able to match a soil sample from the Santa Barbara home he had fled from in the 70s with the soil sample found in his shoes. It turns out he had recently faked a business trip in order to revisit the crime sene on the anniversary of his family's death. Marion and Rosie's local newspaper finally had something big to write about.

48 Movie Madness

During the movie, Martha was a victim of identity theft. John had kept an eye on her in the theatre as promised. Because she placed her coat and handbag on the seat between them, John was able to sneak her social security card, credit cards, and license out of her purse when she was wrapped up in the movie. Martha cancelled her cards and got replacements as soon as she realized, but the damage was already done. John couldn't be located. He had obtained new cards, opened new accounts, and taken out new loans in her name, leaving a trail of unpaid bills that destroyed her credit as well as her husband's. Although Martha was eventually able to resolve her credit problems, it took 600 hours of her time and more than $2,000 to repair the damage that was done.

49 Beer Run

A Breathalyzer test estimates blood alcohol concentration based on several assumptions. One of those assumptions is a normal body temperature of 98.6 degrees. A higher body temperature will cause an overestimation of the actual blood alcohol concentration. The attorney successfully argued that Andrew's rise in body temperature after working most of the day out in the hot sun could have inflated the results of the Breathalyzer test, thus invalidating the results as convincing evidence.

50 Love is Strange

No. Alex sought to rekindle the relationship, not kill Jane. There were no abnormal findings at the scene or upon autopsy. So what killed Jane? Jane's strenuous exercise triggered a fatal heart attack. Her red nail beds and pale skin, her irregular heart beat after strenuous exercise, were evidence of undetected heart disease. Jane's heart developed a deadly change in the normal cardiac rhythm.

51 Love in the Afternoon

The ink on the letter was smudged as though it was feverishly written by a left-handed person. The murder weapon was found on Elaine's left side, which means the killer probably used his left hand to bludgeon her. Elaine was holding the spatula in her right hand, which indicated to the detective that she was right-handed. His presumptions were correct: Elaine's new boyfriend was left-handed. He had written the letter to Nate to try to keep him away from Elaine. When he had later heard Nate's friendly message on the machine, he was convinced that Elaine was cheating on him, so he killed her in a fit of jealous rage.

52 The Cutting Edge

If Ed Morris' knife was the weapon used to kill Linda, and it was thrust deep enough, the hand guard would leave a characteristic mark, or stamp, on the skin surrounding the stab wounds. Because the abrasions on either side of Linda's wound clearly mirrored the hand guard on Ed Morris' knife in size and shape, police were able to positively identify the knife as the murder weapon. Morris was arrested for, and later convicted of, murder.

53 Stealing Tiffany

With Nancy's help, he located the wedding photographer, examined his shots, and learned that the wet young man was seated with Tiffany in his lap before the woman snatched his Yorkie away. The young man was able to prove ownership with the paperwork he had at home, including proof of purchase and veterinary bills that confirmed he was Tiffany's real owner. Yorkshire Terriers like Tiffany are very expensive pets, and are often reported stolen.

54 Party Animals

No. When Drake gave Calvin the noogie, it had been more than just a friendly greeting: He was gathering false evidence. He knew he would kill Veronica that night to teach her a lesson for cheating on him, and he hoped that the hair would divert the police. After stabbing the young girl, he carefully placed the strands of Calvin's hair into her hand. When Calvin unknowingly wandered into the room after the crime occurred, he tripped over Veronica's body and landed in a pool of her blood. Petrified, he went running out the back door. A few days later, the knife was uncovered in a dumpster near Drake's place of work. Once police gathered enough evidence against Drake, Calvin was released.

55 Trouble in Paradise

Their hotel key card was used by a dishonest hotel clerk to commit a series of identity thefts using Harold and Lucy's names. The cards, which look like a credit card, can be used to embed information on the metallic strip along the back that can be read by ATMs and other credit card point-of-sale swipe readers. The type of information on the hotel card strip varies when it's initially stolen, but can include personal information such as home addresses and credit card information. Hotels do not erase the information on the cards until the next guest checks in and the cards are embedded with the new guest's identity. Harold and Lucy were easy targets because they were out of the country while the theft was going on.

56 Highway to Heaven

No. If she didn't know there was a car behind her, she certainly wouldn't have known that the driver was a man. Yet she stated: "I didn't know he was behind me." What makes her story even less convincing is the fact that possums are nocturnal, and wouldn't be out at midday. Betty had become furious with the driver who tailgated her for seven miles and, in an uncharacteristic move, decided to teach him a little lesson about how dangerous tailgating could be. Unfortunately, the man would carry that lesson to his grave, and Betty would have a long time to think about her actions in jail.

57 Stolen Glance

The wear pattern on both shoe print photos was a clear match. Everyone wears out their shoes in a distinct way, depending on where they place the most pressure as they walk. Ned Lester happened to walk heavy on his heels, which was reflected in the shape and texture of the prints his shoes made on the floor. He may have worn different pairs of shoes to the robberies, but he committed both of them.

58 The Test of Time

Gilbert was careful and creative in planning and executing the theft of antique books that, until recently, wouldn't have seemed valuable. But he made one big mistake: When he examined the fakes that he commissioned page by page, he inadvertently left a latent index fingerprint on one of the bindings. This latent print might not have suggested Gilbert's guilt, except that it was the only print the examiner found, suggesting that it had been left either by the forger or the thief. Either way, Gilbert was a suspect. A careful comparison of the latent print with an exemplar print from Gilbert when the museum's employees were required to submit prints for exclusion purposes, pointed to Gilbert.

59 Crystal Clear

The ice crystals were crucial in discovering the cause of death. While a body left out in the cold for a while will freeze from the outside in, the ice crystals in Mary's heart revealed that she was frozen only on the inside. Because water expands when cold, the large size of the crystals suggests that she was slowly frozen and had only recently thawed. This explained the fresh appearance of the corpse, the visible year-old cuts on her legs and the relative lack of damage to the exterior of her body. Mary was abducted on her way home and suffocated shortly afterward. The water in her heart expanded when she was left inside a freezer, where she was kept for most of the year.

60 Making Scents of It All

A .38 caliber gun is the kind most often used by law enforcement officers, including security guards. Rick was a security guard at the mall's aromatherapy store before he was fired for stealing. He had learned in his brief time working there that the scent of black licorice was supposed to be a turn on for women. When Maggie rejected Mr. Wrong and his scent, they quarreled and he shot her twice at point blank range.

61 One of a Kind

Brian noticed what appeared to be Felix's grimy ear print on the glass panel of the closed bathroom door. Felix had broken in just hours earlier and put his ear to the door to hear whether Nadine was in the shower. When Felix realized she wasn't there, he ran out. Brian and Nadine showed the ear print to police, but the police were skeptical that it could implicate Felix. The uniqueness of the human ear as a basis for identification is disputed. While the human ear is probably different for each person, experts may not be able to differentiate one ear from another by observing the ear's external gross anatomy. Due to the absence of something particularly identifiable about the ear print, such as a mole, tear, scar, or unusual shape, Felix was never charged.

62 Not My Type

No. While blood typing sometimes determines that someone is not the father in question, it can not match a specific father to a specific son in the way that DNA testing can. For example, if Dylan's son has type O blood and Dylan has type AB blood, then blood typing would confirm that he's not the father. But if Dylan has type A blood, he might be the father depending on whether he has the recessive O gene. Even if he does have type A blood with genotype AO, there are plenty of other men out there with the same type of blood who could also be the boy's father. Because a child's DNA contains only those DNA fragments provided by his parents, experts can confirm paternity by ensuring that the DNA profile of the child contains fragments specific to the parents in question. If a fragment of Dylan's child's DNA cannot be accounted for by looking at Dylan and the real mother's DNA, then Dylan is not the father. In general, about 30 percent of paternity tests come back negative, meaning that the claimed father of the child is not the biological father. Sadly enough, Dylan's tests also came back negative. He sued the child's mother for extortion and won.

63 Life Sentence

The autopsy ruled cause of death as asthma, but the condition alone hadn't killed Arlene. Knowing that Arlene was particularly sensitive to sawdust, Gregory had blown some of the sawdust leftover from his woodworking projects into their home to aggravate her condition and drive her to an earlier grave.

64 Falling for Her

Yes. If both footprints faced the edge of the cliff, Brandon couldn't have fallen backwards over the edge as Shelly claimed. Brandon had come onto Shelly when they were alone. He had pulled her tight to him near the edge of the cliff. She broke loose and pushed him away. He lost his balance and fell forward over the edge. Shelly was afraid she'd be charged with murder, even though it was an accident, so she lied to the police.

65 Digging Up the Past

The body of a drowning victim will float due to gasses created as the body decomposes, but the water temperature has a significant effect on how quickly a body fills up with gasses.

In warmer waters, a body may float after just a few days or a week, but when submerged in colder water, it can take weeks or months for a body to rise to the water's surface. Sandy had described the water as 'frigid.' In frigid water, her father's body would not have been seen floating after only a day or two as the author declared. Clearly, the author had lied about finding the body, but he did direct police to its exact location near the lake. How is this possible? The man who murdered Sandy's father in the seventies was the author of the anonymous letter. It had always bothered him that the body of his first victim was never found. He had carried out what he considered the perfect murder—one clean shot to the head—and no one would ever appreciate it. Thirty years later, he took the risk of writing Sandy the letter, knowing that the body would be unearthed and he would finally get the recognition he deserved.

ABOUT THE AUTHOR

Diane Capri is an award-winning and international best-selling author. She turned to writing fiction after practicing law. She writes for the same reason she reads, to find out what happens next. Learn more about Diane and her work at https://dianecapri.com/